For Heaven's Sake

MY STORY
Part Two

John Edwards

PUBLISHING

First published in 2015 by MDP
www.malcolmdown.co.uk

www.walkingfree.org

British Library Cataloguing in Publication Data
A catalogue record of this book is available from the British
Library
ISBN: 978-1-910786-11-6

Scripture quotations are taken from The Holy Bible, New
International Version (Anglicised edition). Copyright ©1979,
1984, 2011 by Biblica (formerly International Bible Society). Used
by permission of Hodder & Stoughton Publishers, an Hachette UK
company. All rights reserved.

Author's note: Out of consideration for friends and families
I have, in some instances, changed the names of persons
mentioned in this book.

Cover design by Rebecca Stewart
Printed and bound by CPI Group
(UK) Ltd, Croydon, CR0 4YY

Contents

Dedication

I dedicate this book to the memory of my mother Alice and sister Evelyn, both of whom died during the writing of this book. I miss you both so much.

Acknowledgements

I am so grateful to all my friends who have willingly volunteered their help and continued to cheer me on as I write and reach out to others. My friends Bob and Jane Baker, also Sean and Julia O'Mahony, your gift of help with punctuation, proofreading and editing blessed me. Thanks to Eddie and Beckie Stewart who designed the book cover. I want to give special thanks to my family, especially to Tricia my amazing wife, for supporting me during the writing of this book. I love you all.

Foreword

God 'has set eternity in the human heart' (Ecclesiastes 3:11). John Edwards is such a man whose eternity has been unlocked by Christ. Having found that freedom, John has not only triumphed over unspeakable and horrendous odds, but has gone on to help many others find their new life in Christ as well. John's life story is a miraculous example of the saving grace of Jesus Christ and proves that there is so much more to eternity than life after death. John's life is proof that we can have life before death. To see John flourishing and enjoying life with his wife Tricia and to see them both as a vibrant part of our local church is such a joy.

What God can do for one, he can do for anyone. If God can deliver one from drug addiction, he can do it for another. If God can help one overcome past mistakes and find the strength to help them move forward, he can do it for you; to help people who are far from God and who are often in the grips of great discouragement to discover eternity. It takes courage to undertake a journey that will require you to move past personal hurt and heartache, so that you can plunge into the oceans of God's forgiveness and grace. These oceans of forgiveness and grace are so vast that it will take the rest of eternity for humankind to appreciate their worth.

Eternity is so much more than what you are saved from; it is what you are saved for. Finding out what you are saved for is like firing up a jet engine and taking flight for the first time. You suddenly become aware not only of the theory of flight but of the exhilaration and thrill of becoming airborne. Helping people understand and connect with what they are saved to do is to help them discover their destinies and take flight.

In order to understand eternity in others and to help people move from hurt to health, an essential ingredient is needed: compassion. When compassion combines with courage it produces such a powerful force that even the most destitute respond. I have seen John help many who others would say that there is no hope for. I have seen him in recent years sleep nights on the streets of Bradford, the city to our local church, in the peak of winter. Why? So that he can better remember what God has saved him from and to remind himself to what God has saved him for. Why would anyone do that? Compassion.

Compassion taught is never as powerful as compassion demonstrated and imparted. When you have compassion you will gain the insight you need to unlock eternity in others. Jesus had compassion, wept and then raised Lazarus from the dead (John 11:1–43). Many years ago I heard the phrase 'people don't care how much you know, until they know how much you care'.

In my ministry I have found that to be so true. Emotion alone is not enough. Feelings come and go, but compassion will fuel you to action and sustain you reaching people for the rest of your life. Do you have enough compassion to motivate you to action to do something about the eternal state of the people you know and the strangers you bump into along the journey of life?

Eternity need not be one of the most confused, misunderstood or neglected parts of the human condition. Instead, it should be unlocked through courageous conversations and great compassion.

I am so encouraged to have a friend like John Edwards, who serves as a constant reminder of what God has done and a provocation about what God will do when we reach out to others. I pray that as you read this book it will show you your potential, unlocking power of eternity in the hearts of those around you every day.

Steve Gambill
Lead Pastor, LIFE Church UK

A Word From
Mark Stevens...

To me, John Edwards is a living legend, plain and simple. His testimony is nothing short of breathtaking ... for me it's comparable to an epic blockbuster movie. I often marvel at the things John has experienced. Most people would've thrown in the towel and called it quits, but not John! He seems to live life on a daily basis that defies the odds ... that defies even death itself. This is no exaggeration.

I first met John about ten years ago and was instantly impacted by him as a person. He carried such a strength and authority which was tempered by a peace that has weathered all kinds of storms. I was intrigued ... I loved being around him to glean from his wisdom and experience. Since then I have become a close friend ... and can now say, a best friend.

More recently I stood next to John and his wife Trish during a season when John was receiving chemotherapy for hepatitis C. I watched my friend's body literally waste away, but I was amazed to witness his faith in Christ get stronger and stronger. Yet again John had stared death in the face and beaten it. John has now been told that the hepatitis C is non-detectable, which really means it has completely disappeared from his body! Hallelujah!

To me John is generous to a fault, authentically real, non-religious, inspiring, encouraging and daring. He is willing to display a life in Christ that is far from normal, living a life completely outside of the box! He dares to step into unknown terrain almost daily. Some call him crazy but I call him one of my deepest friends.

John, I love you man .... I know this book is going to change lives and impact people for eternity!

I know, reader, that as you open these pages you will be encouraged by a man that not only talks the talk, but walks the walk!

Mark Stevens
Worship Leader

Chapter 1
Goodbye Evelyn

It's raining outside. I'm sitting in Dublin Airport at Gate 19 waiting for a plane to Leeds Bradford Airport, England. The radar is down in Dublin and a long wait is guaranteed. Commuters exercise unusual restraint as monotonous bulletins echo news of flights delayed or cancelled. We all have hours to wait. Everyone resigns themselves to wait patiently.

Now, however, decisions have to be made on how best to pass the time. Being a frequent traveller I am used to delayed flights and long airport waiting times. I take the opportunity to indulge in my favourite pastime of people watching, reading faces, observing how they manage tired and hyperactive kids. I marvel at how people put a cap on their anger. How they patiently practise uncommon restraint and postpone arguments with their partners and kids just because they're going on holiday and they don't want to ruin it when they haven't even left the airport yet. Thousands of tired and travel-weary travellers find ingenious ways to amuse themselves. Laptops, Kindles, books and smartphones are taken out and DVDs put on.

One family near me is huddling round a game of Scrabble. Lone travellers, small families and couples gather round their compact computers to watch films they had kept for rainy days or the odd night in on holiday. Wi-Fi is free, so some surf the Net. Two kids are playing on an airport trolley. They are making a racket that normally would not be tolerated in an airport but tonight there is an unspoken agreement to be extra patient because, after all, we're in this delay together.

Four Asian men are lying on the hard tiled floor at the edge of the airport gate corridor; resting their heads on their jackets, they sleep. One of them is snoring slightly, just loud enough to be heard. A young girl is smiling at him. I guess she thinks it's funny. She catches me looking at her, I smile back. She hunches up her shoulders and smiles an even broader smile, showing off her lovely white teeth. I can tell by the well-dressed, middle class look of the Asian guys that sleeping rough like this is foreign to them. There's homeless survival mode in all of us, I thought. If they were dressed in ragged old clothes with a bottle of wine beside them they would be put out of the building.

This is amazing; a sense of community welfare is developing. Some people are buying each other tea, coffee and other drinks. Strangers are talking to one another like they have known each other for ages. The airport radar crisis has caused thousands of people to find common ground – they're all friendly now.

I notice, though, that a few are not joining in. They sit apart, with their heads in a book, or just daydreaming. Others look forlorn or worried, their faces taut and furrows creasing their brows. Their minds are obviously elsewhere. They look like they have given up on that important business meeting or date with fiancé, family or friends.

I chat for a while with the girl sitting beside me. Her name is Georgina. She is on her way to meet her boyfriend in Yorkshire. I offer to buy her a cup of tea, thinking to myself, 'I might as well join the radar-down phenomenon of airport friendliness.' Georgina agrees to let me buy her a cup of tea. As I walk down the long corridor to fetch our drinks I notice a group of young folk looking after some old people, making sure they are comfortable. There are no arguments about planes being late, just a quiet resignation to the fact that the radar is down. I think how inspiring it is to see people showing kindness to each other.

After buying tea for Georgina I return to my seat and begin to reflect on my week at home in Dublin. Evelyn, my dear, elder sister, was suffering with alcoholism and was very sick. She had had a terrific battle with cancer and broken her hip previously. Alcohol was taking out its brutal and savage wrath on this beautiful, kind girl, my sister. Camouflaged by alcohol addiction, disguised as drink-fuelled sickness, cancer had crept in unnoticed. Its deadly grip had invaded her unsuspecting body with its hellish, hateful claws.

She'd finally stopped drinking, turning her attentions to attempt recovery. She had battled for over a year. A kidney had been removed and a growth taken off her lung. Then half her teeth and gums were taken out before the cancer attacked her leg and head. Now, having fought like a champion, she was bowing her brave efforts to the unforgiving, unrelenting claws of death. They were gripping her and I had to watch, not understanding why God hadn't healed her. She still had so much in her to give to others. Her wealth was in her beautiful ability to give to others unconditionally. What an awful waste it would be if she died without giving more of the loving assets still left in her heart.

I knew that God heals cancer – I'd seen it, experienced it even. Evelyn weighed only four-and-a-half stone now. Her leg had snapped. She screamed in pain when it happened. It seemed that it, too, was full of cancer. Strange, she was calmer now, serene even; she had a sense of the presence of God about her. I believe she had an encounter with God just a few months earlier. She had limped into the bathroom of her apartment in Dublin's suburb; the painkillers she had been prescribed were not taking the excruciating pain away from her cancer-riddled body. She clung onto the washbasin and, while she looked in the mirror at her cancer-ravaged reflection, she called out to God with everything within her. Suddenly the presence of God filled the bathroom and filled her entire being as well. She phoned me later to tell me about it. 'The pain left me immediately, John,' she said, 'then God's presence and peace flooded my entire being. I know what you mean now,' she said, 'when you speak so fervently about God coming into your life.'

I had spent the last week visiting her at the hospice. I purposely made memories, just sitting with her, talking, and reminiscing over our past. We even played a game of poker with her friends in the hospice. All of them had cancer or some other terminal illness. Playing poker with Evelyn was a trip down memory lane for both of us. We used to play in poker classics years ago, quite successfully too. Funny, poker is like riding a bike: you never forget. I fleeced them all, and won a fortune, although it was only for plastic chips. Evelyn laughed with me, 'You've no mercy, John. You'd think you'd pity us all here, what with us all being sick! You're ruthless!' she said, giving me a weak poke in my side with her bony knuckle. I liked that!

Within just a few days the palliative morphine care the hospital was administering to her was having its way with her body and mind, slowly affecting her breathing. Her body was slowing down. Long day-time and night-time sleep was coming easily. Conversation had become tiring for her. For Evelyn the battle was nearing its early end. Her fighting spirit was losing and, although she was yielding, I was still praying.

Late that night while she was sleeping, I sneaked quietly into her hospice room. The staff let me in. I had come to say my last goodbye before heading home to Yorkshire. I wanted to have my special moment with Ev. She had stuck with me through the toughest of times in my own life, never leaving me, never giving up hope for me. Her tiny frame lay in the bed, her body smaller than a child's, her face serene as she lay in her morphine sleep. I sat down in the wheelchair next to Evelyn's bed. I gently put my hand on hers and pleaded with God to heal her. The kind, sensitive hospice staff wheeled in a leather recliner chair and a little lamp for me so I could rest and stay as long as I wanted. I believe they sensed that this was a special moment for me, that I had come to say my last goodbye.

I relaxed into the recliner chair, reached out my hand again so I could rest it gently on Evelyn's as she slept. I put my iPod on and listened to some lovely worship music. I was willing the presence of God to come and touch her while I allowed myself to go back and remember good times I'd had with her. I knew that I would not be here now if it hadn't been for Ev; she had been my saviour so many times, never giving up on me. Ev had always given so much, not just to me but to everyone who came across her path. An angel couldn't have done more for me than Evelyn. I thought of her kindness, patience and relentless spirit. Although she had not had an easy life, her thoughtful nature always gave and caused her to be there for others.

I held her hand tighter, so wanting to let her know I loved her and that I was here, yet still not wanting to wake her. Looking at her she looked spent; she was on the home-run in the race of life. I leant over her and whispered in her ear, saying, 'It's time to go home to heaven now, Ev.'

While I was leaning over her I noticed a book on her bedside cabinet. Picking it up I saw that it was a book describing heaven. Wow, I thought, she was reading and checking out the reality of heaven, like someone browsing a map before they go on a journey. I don't cry very often but I have to admit that tears brimmed over just then. I was delighted that heaven was on her mind and that now for my lovely sister going home to heaven was nearing reality. The pain was worth it; the wait, the struggles, the hard times, they were all worth it.

I lay back in the recliner seat, relaxed my hold on Evelyn's hand a little and thought about heaven. I imagined joining her there one day, what a joyful reunion that will be! I quietly thanked God that he had provided a way for all of us to go there through Jesus Christ; without his death on the cross none of us would be going there. I am sure I am going to heaven and I was now convinced that Evelyn was going there too.

I have been to heaven. Yes, it's true, I've been there. It's fresh in my mind, just as if it was yesterday. I was just think-ing about it again last night. It seems that there has never been an author who could fully describe heaven. Even the apostle John in the book of Revelation didn't satisfy us as to what heaven will be like for us. But first I was to experience the darkest of times.

Chapter 2
Light in My Darkness

Tricia and I had been happily married for about three years. We were still living in Largs, a beautiful seaside town on the west coast of Scotland; in fact we were in the same house I mentioned in part one of my autobiography, *Walking Free*.

I was working in a church on the Ayrshire coast, reaching out to and helping addicts, alcoholics and their families. Word travelled fast and as local people spread the word about the help we were offering, people in need began to come to us. It seemed to me that the whole county of Ayrshire had heard about the work.

Every morning I would go to work and there would be a group of addicts waiting for me. Sometimes they would bring their parents or friends. Often there were up to nine or ten of these sad, addicted people looking for help. I had to put chairs in the corridor outside my office for them while they waited. One by one I brought them into my office where I would talk, listen and pray with them. Many were helped during this time. It was really quite remarkable. Within a short time we had twenty-five young men and women in rehabilitation centres such as Teen Challenge and Victory Outreach. Still they came, every day, more and more of them. I began to rent safe flats and houses for them. Within a few months I had rented eleven properties, each of which had to be furnished and food bought for the occupants. Housing benefit helped pay the rents but I had to raise the deposits and other money myself. I did this by preaching around the country. Kind, caring and sympathetic people also supported the work, and the church helped us financially.

But we needed to find employment for them. So with the help of my friend and pastor of the church, Terry Quinn, we opened a café for them to work in, and a car valeting business.

My office was no longer big enough to accommodate the numbers of people that came to us for help so we rented a large house near the church. I called this house The Haven. I used to say it was our 'haven in the midst of havoc'. This gave me plenty of room to look after the many that came to us. I had my office on one side of the house. Adjoining was a big room where the addicts who were serious about getting their lives together would come.

I had strict policies and firm boundaries to help protect the work and to ensure the safety and progress of those who were trying to get and stay clean. A local doctor worked with me to help detox the addicts. Many came to me who were on a lot of heroin or methadone. The local doctor was willing to do whatever he could to help me help the addicts. He was caring, had time for the addicts, and wanted to help them get their lives back on track. We detoxed them quickly on dihydrocodeine, which is also an opiate (a drug containing opium used to ease pain) and with the help of prayer we saw many set free from high doses of heroin and methadone.

I get frustrated with the length of time it takes government agencies to detox someone from heroin, methadone or any other drug. They are so over the top in Health and Safety that they have ruined detox for many. They don't seem to understand the mind-set of the addict. Long detoxes that the government offer, by and large, in my opinion and experience, do not work. The temptation to take other drugs while doing a long detox is too much and nearly all of the time the addict will fall back to using their drugs of choice again. Government agencies that work with addicts are often not helping the individual at all. Indeed I would go as far as to say they often make the problem worse. They increase the amount of methadone an addict is using for no reason at all. This leads to more addiction to the methadone than they had to the heroin they were initially addicted to. Then if they get a dirty urine sample (urine with traces of drugs in it) the addict will be told they will be cut down or have their methadone stopped. It's a sad and awful system of control and it's killing many young men and women.

Government agencies don't allow us to use the word addict anymore either. They claim it may be upsetting or offensive to the person addicted to drugs. They insist on calling the addict a 'service user' and of course they are 'service providers'. This is a complete load of nonsense; I am a former addict, not a former service user. Unless an addict admits he or she is an addict – that is, that they are actually addicted to drugs, alcohol, etc. – they will not recover. Then they must become willing to do whatever it takes to get and stay clean. Only then will they have any chance of recovery.

We were able to detox an addict within one to three weeks, sometimes within days. Some went cold turkey (came straight off drugs without medical help). We prayed with them and saw many miracles happen. Entire families who were addicted came for help too. I remember one family in particular. The mum, dad and four kids, all heroin users or addicts, were helped. The parents had been drug dealers and the children used to steal the heroin and smoke it. They were only kids; one of them was only ten years of age. The weight of responsibility was huge, the pressure great. Looking back I can now see that it was more than I could manage – hindsight is a perfect science.

Pastors, leaders and others came from around the country to see our work. The Glasgow drug squad came to learn from us and to support us in the making of drugs education videos. I came to an agreement with the Glasgow police that if I got any guns, knives or other weapons from addicts that the police would safely dispose of them for me without charging the addicts. The condition was that none of the weapons had been used in serious crime. I have walked through the area, carrying a gun in my pocket and the bullets in the other pocket. I would then meet the police and hand the weapons over without a word being said. I had huge knives, machetes and other weapons hidden in a big box in my house; we disposed of them too.

Schools, prisons and youth clubs asked me to come and teach them or speak about drugs and addiction. It was a hectic time.

In some Christian circles they would call this 'revival' or 'a move of God'. There was indeed a terrific sense of the presence of God around us during that time. Newspapers reported on the work and printed stories of how the addicts were getting clean. The local police called into my office one day to thank us for the work we were doing. They said that since we had come to town the crime rate had dropped dramatically.

Tricia was marvellous; she cooked, cleaned, mothered

them and generally just loved on them. You see, when the flats and houses we had rented were full, we used to take people into our home to look after them, detox them and just plain love on them.

Tricia's teenage children, Kevin, Paul, Lianne and Amanda – now my stepchildren – were fabulous. Sometimes they gave up their beds for these lost, hurting and addicted people; they befriended them and treated them with love and respect.

Tricia had looked after local hurting children all her life and this showed in the caring attitude her children had inherited. I would often be out late at night, visiting addicts and helping them with the problems that come with their lifestyle. It must be said here that often the families of the addicts needed help and support too. The parents worried about their kids. They would relate to me the heart-breaking stories addiction brought to their homes. Some of these families struggled by on benefits. The added problems an addicted child brought to their homes was often unbearable for them. The siblings of the addict would also struggle. Sometimes they joined their brother or sister in drug-taking, becoming addicted themselves. Trying to break this cycle is difficult but I am delighted to say that we were able to offer comfort, support and sometimes practical help to these families.

Some critical people would tell me that the addicts I was working with were not worth it, that they were hopeless cases and that they would never get clean. 'Put them in prison and throw the key away,' they would say. My motto was that I would never give up on them. Where others left them and didn't believe in them, I would stick with them until they came through into freedom. Sadly, some didn't make it. I attended, sometimes officiated, at several funerals during this time, and often to hold the ropes around the coffins as their bodies were lowered into their final resting place. I was satisfied, though, that I had shared the gospel with them and prayed with them. My hope was always to lead them to Christ, so that if they did die they would go to heaven.

I am sure you can imagine the strain our lives were under. I was exhausted. The ministry was taking its toll on me. I began to burn out and my mental energy was almost gone. Every day became a great effort. God was moving. Addicts were getting helped, saved and sent to rehab, but I was going downhill fast. Every morning I would wake and feel a terrible hole or ache in my stomach; I had to drag myself out of bed and force myself to go to work every day. Tricia was worried about me. She knew I was doing too much, that the work was taking its toll on me. She always encouraged me but, deep down, she too was being worn down by the stress of it all.

I normally took a day off every week but during this time it was almost impossible to do so. Sometimes I worked twenty hours or more a day. I now know that working like this is a set up for burnout, especially when one is working with seriously dysfunctional people. I heard a counsellor use the term 'Psychic Debris' once to describe the baggage that sticks to your soul when working with dysfunctional people. This is a good term and describes well the draining weight of stress and concern that addicts have on your life. I believe this is the reason that there are not many people who survive – and I use the word 'survive' on purpose – after working with addicted, dysfunctional people for many years.

I longed for a break, for some normal life, for a holiday with Tricia. We loved each other so much, but the work was getting to be too much. I wasn't coping well at all. Our marriage began to feel the strain. On top of this there were terrible struggles amongst some of the leaders in our church. I was aware of some of it but I did not have the experience nor could I find the energy to turn my attention to it. I don't believe that I would have been able to help very much; this was an area of our church life that I wasn't caught up in. I find it interesting that because I was busy reaching out to lost and hurting people I was not involved in internal affairs and church politics. I trusted the other guys to manage these things well. How wrong I was.

Some of the leaders began to complain about the amount of addicts coming to the church. 'We're turning into an addict's church,' some of them complained. I understood their concerns and sympathised with them, however my allegiance was to the addicts and their families. The momentum was such that it would have been very difficult to stop what had been started by God. It was not like there were only addicts in our church; there were over a hundred and twenty reasonably well-healed middle class people in our church as well as kids and teenagers. I saw the big picture and I knew that one day some of these addicts would work in this area and help others.

Dealers Set Free

Let me tell you about one of the many amazing break-throughs we had during this time.

One morning an addict named Andrew came to meet me. He was not only an addict but he was also one of the main drug dealers in the area. There was a heroin famine at the time he came to see me. We chatted in my office for a while and when we finished chatting and sharing about God he left to go about his business. He was a little dubious regarding God and had not come to a place of trusting in him yet.

I walked Andrew out to the car park adjacent to our

church. He drove a sporty white car, a typical drug deal-
er's car. He turned the ignition key but the engine would
not start. I said to him that if I laid hands on the car it
might start. I was kidding him but at the same time I was
half serious. He laughed with me and said, 'That would be
a miracle.'

I laid my hands on the roof of his drug-dealer car and
prayed, 'God, please make Andrew's car work, in Jesus'
name.'

'Try the car now, Andrew,' I said. He turned the ignition
key again and the car started first time. Coincidence?
Maybe, but it had an impact on Andrew.

About a week later Andrew came back to my office
and told me he had arranged for several of the local drug
dealers to come round to his house. 'John, I want you to
come round to my home to speak to us all as we are so
sick of our addictions and want freedom. Will you come
round?' he pleaded.

I jumped at the chance, 'Of course I'll come round,
Andrew,' I answered. The meeting was arranged in
Andrew's house for the next Friday. This could be the
breakthrough I had been praying for. You see, if you can
get the dealers saved and free you can do some serious
damage to the local drug trade.

That next Friday I went to Andrew's house. It must be
said I was a little nervous. I wondered how they would
receive me. Would they listen or would they reject me and
the message I brought? That was the big question.

Andrew lived in a three-bedroom council house. I
knocked at the front door, and he answered immediately.
The second I walked in Andrew locked the door behind
me. Now that made me a little nervous! 'Go on through to
the living room, John,' he directed.

It was a messy room. Eight or nine of the local dealers

were lounging around. Some sat on the floor, while others sat either on the couch or leant against the wall by the kitchen. There was a visible cloud of smoke in the room, a mix from them smoking heroin, hash and cigarettes. The smell was intoxicating. 'Do you mind opening a window please, Andrew?' I asked. 'If you don't I'll get stoned and be unable to talk coherently to you!' They all laughed at this statement of mine. Andrew opened a window; his next sentence blew me away.

'Guys,' he said, 'this is John. I told you that he had a fresh batch of smack [heroin] for us, but the truth is John is a Christian; he is an ex-addict too. I have asked him to come round to talk to us about getting clean.'

'What?! Are you ******* mad, Andrew,' they said. 'We were expecting him to have smack for us!'

I was not prepared for this. Knowing that the front door was locked I began frantically looking for a way out. Glancing at the window I contemplated jumping if things got out of hand. I decided against it and stood my ground. 'Come on, guys,' Andrew said, 'let's give John a chance to talk to us. We're all sick of our addiction. We've talked many times about how we want to change our lives and get clean. At least give him a few minutes to speak to us.'

Finally, after much shouting and cursing they agreed to listen to me. 'We'll give John ten minutes to speak to us!'

I nervously introduced myself, and then I spoke on addiction, explaining the process of detox I used for local addicts. Eventually sharing my story I told them clearly and boldly that Christ could and would set them free if they were willing to ask God to come into their lives.

Unbelievably, they all agreed. I will never forget that moment! What a privilege it was to lead all the local dealers in prayer to Christ. I spoke for forty minutes in total. Today one of those guys is a Church of Scotland minister. He has a degree in theology and pastors a church near Edinburgh. He now has a beautiful wife and lovely child. Others from amongst them are married and settled down. One looks after her elderly blind mother. Another has worked in prisons sharing the gospel. Andrew now pastors a church in the area and runs a rehab alongside it. Most of the dealers in the room that day are now clean and living good Christian lives. Hallelujah!

So you see there were amazing things happening. Behind the scenes, though, there was an extreme amount of work to do in leading these people to freedom. Sometimes they went to rehab but were unable to stay on task with the programme and left. I then had to work alongside them to get them to return. On and on it went, until I could get as many of them through into freedom. It sometimes took years of persevering to get them through to real freedom.

Chapter 3
My Near-fatal Mistake

The work with the addicts continued to be exhausting and very strenuous, it didn't help that the leadership struggles in our church were coming to a head. I was trying to deal with burnout, then in the midst of my exhaustion I made a terrible mistake. In hindsight I should have seen it coming.

Some of the addicts were detoxing so quickly that they were finishing their prescribed medication early. My policy was always to either throw these medications out or return them to chemist shops. However, a few Librium ended up in the bottom of my desk drawer. I had intended to throw them out but in the midst of business and pressure I didn't. One day, whilst under intense pressure, I took one of the Librium to ease the strain a little. This was a stupid mistake on my part. I felt guilty taking it but I convinced myself that it was just for one day. The next day I took another, then the following day I took two. That was a bad idea; within a few weeks I came very close to falling back into addiction.

I was amazed at how quickly I found myself falling back into the thinking of an addict. I almost lost it all. I knew that if I didn't stop I could lose all the freedom I had gained over the last ten years. I learned a huge lesson through this experience.

I hear former addicts giving testimonies about how God has set them free from their addictions. They often say that they will never return to the life they once lived. I am now twenty-two years into my recovery and I have learned that I must always be careful. I must never become complacent. Humility and brokenness have taught me that addiction will patiently wait for an opportunity to try and take me out again.

You may not know this, but there are addicts, and there are long-term addicts. Short-term addicts (people who have experienced addiction for just a few years) meet certain obstacles in their journey to recovery. But people who have had long-term, serious addiction, for ten to thirty years or more, meet obstacles that short-term addicts do not have to face. Be warned if you are a former addict reading this: do not become complacent; watch for signs of burnout that can become so destructive. I learned that there are roots of addiction and addictive behaviour that it takes years to pull out. I have also learned that a man with my background cannot take medication to ease the pressure or strain of life. People like us must stay away completely from alcohol, strong painkillers, sleeping pills, tranquilisers and antidepressants. Addicts and alcoholics: you break this rule at your peril – be warned! You could and may lose everything again if you breach these boundaries.

I prayed much during this time and by the grace of God I managed to pull myself together and focus on getting well.

It seems to me that if the devil cannot get you any other way he will push you so hard that he will try to destroy you. That is what was happening to me.

I have also learned that there is a phenomenon that happens to many of us at the stage when we are about ten- to twelve-years clean. Perhaps we get too self-assured or we compromise, but many of us have a slip during this stage. I thank my God that he helped me during this time. Former addicts often have a destructive pride that stops them from sharing their problems; this can be fatal. We must have lifestyles that are a little different from other so-called normal people. The pride that says I can have a drink or I can take addictive medication when it is not really necessary is the rock on which we can slowly perish. I thank God for the humbling experience I had while learning this lesson and I pray others will take note too.

There are consequences to bad decisions and I was about to suffer exaggerated accusations and lies that resulted from my near fall. Yet I can say with confidence, 'What a faithful God we serve!' Tricia and I took some much-needed time out to rest and for me to recover from my close call and burnout.

There was another crisis looming in the background though. While I was taking my break our church began to fall apart. There was compromise on the part of the pastor. Yet instead of wise discipline and a restoration process taking place, the leadership went on what I can only describe as a crusade of destruction. It is not my place or job to go into all the details of the church troubles, except to say that the pastor and others involved in the church at that time were treated disgracefully. I was not included in the dialogue regarding the inner-church struggles and to a large degree I was unaware of them.

It was during this time that my friend Gordon and I travelled to the USA on our first attempt to walk across the country. Tricia came to London with Gordon's wife Helen to see us off on our mission. I knew that this break was exactly what I needed to get myself back on my feet. That trip was amazing; I'll share about it a little later in the book.

During my six weeks away when the church began to fall apart, the leadership nearly destroyed the pastor and others during this time. Unfortunately, the church came close to total collapse.

The leadership then turned and made some amazing accusations against me. I hadn't shared with any of them about my near-fatal slip on medication; I didn't trust them. I had only shared it with my spiritual father Mr Hugh Black and with Jay Fallon. Jay is now the national director of Teen Challenge in Britain. I shared with them for support and for the sake of accountability.

Tricia and I received wise council from Mr Black during this time. Hindsight begs the question: was it right not to share my slip with the leaders at the time? I believe even now fifteen years later that I made the right decision. When the accusations against me began to surface I was not even in the country to answer for myself.

They pulled Tricia into the drama of their confusion, distortion, lies and deception. They accused me of being on heroin, of having an affair with a staff member of the church, as well as other unmentionable things. I see no benefit in going into them now except to say that they were complete lies and demonic distortions of the truth.

When I returned from the USA after six weeks, I found out about the accusations against me. I could not believe the lies – I was devastated. To prove I was drug free I paid weekly visits to the doctor for urine sample testing. I kept the results on file to prove to anyone who questioned me that I was completely drug free.

Roots of rejection from my past began to surface; my response was one of survival. I wanted to run, and I was ill-equipped, not having the needed experience to fight this battle. I looked within to find the strength to fight but unfortunately I didn't find it.

I convinced myself during this time that I was not called by God to be an evangelist or even a worker in the Christian field. I told myself that maybe I was a bad person. I knew I was not perfect and never would be; I could see many weaknesses and character defects within and I judged myself accordingly. Learning to apply grace to everyone else, I had forgotten to apply it to myself. Over twenty years of addiction and homelessness had taught me how to become used to people looking down on me. During the past ten years I had earned the respect of many and had worked hard to get a better life. My self-esteem was now leaking right out of my boots; I guess I was on a destructive pity party.

Overall, though, I knew that I would come through this. I had learned enough in life as a Christian to know that somehow God would bring me out the far side; I knew that one day I would be able to see the benefit of these trials and that, no matter what, I would grow as a person. I seriously tried to practise grace towards everyone at this time; it was all I knew to do. I knew that to become bitter or angry would only bring me down. Survival told me this situation was bigger than anything I could manage on my own so I spent long days on the hills near my house praying and seeking God. The serenity prayer I had learned at Alcoholics Anonymous meetings was special to me during these times:

God grant me the serenity to accept the things I cannot change, give me the courage to change the things I can and the wisdom to know the difference.

I began to look for regular employment. I applied for many jobs, anything, just so I could provide for my family. Day after day I would fill in applications for jobs but I didn't get one positive answer. I was feeling very sorry for myself. Night after night I would lie awake, tormented by the thoughts of inadequacy and hopelessness, battling against the temptation to become bitter. I could not rid myself of the tormenting thoughts that assailed me on a daily basis: they were overwhelming and destructive. God, I prayed, please give me some peace. I longed for peace but it wasn't coming.

I began to have suicidal thoughts, something I had never considered before in my life. I tried without much success to push these thoughts to one side. I'm a stubborn person, though, and I refused to give in to these thoughts. I dug deep and prayed in faith for God to help me. I now understand that suggestions of suicide lurk around the arena of hopelessness. These destructive thoughts wait to strike us in the darkness that permeates the atmosphere when we are at our lowest and when we believe we don't have the ability to fight or navigate impossible situations.

In my past I survived well while living on the streets and in rat-infested squats. I've been in psychiatric hospitals, padded cells, and been abused in every imaginable way, overdosing over twenty times and being left for dead after being beaten up. But never, in all of that, had I been hurt the way I was during this time.

I tried to be an example of what a Christian man of God is meant to be when accusations are made against him. I had to, for survival's sake. For the sake of the others I was working with and for my family's sake, I had to. I bought books on surviving the onslaught of the enemy and on the trials that other Christians had suffered. I bought a book from Mr Black's church bookshop called Crucified by Christians by Gene Edwards. That book literally saved my life; I recommend it to anyone going through serious spiritual abuse or who is in a dysfunctional church situation. During this time Mr Black made many references in his preaching to how I was being treated. He didn't mention my name of course. He was my spiritual tower of strength during this time and I thank God for him.

I found much comfort in the Scriptures, in which I saw how Jesus was accused, beaten, punched, bruised and even hung on a cross until dead. He had never sinned, was never in the wrong, yet humans treated our Saviour this way. I was amazed to realise that he was never vindicated until after he died. It was only after Jesus died that the centurion said, 'Surely he is the Son of God.' In other words, even Jesus had to die to the need for vindication.

I desperately wanted someone, anyone, to say something encouraging to me or give me good news ... I could not sense the presence of God near me. I thought that maybe he was angry with me. I searched my soul and asked God to find any offensive way in me. Then I sought to die to self so I could find a way through this pain. 'God,' I'd cry, 'please be real to me. I need you so much, please come and help me.' I'd climb into my room in the loft of my house, my cave as I called it, and call out to God to hear me.

One day, unexpectedly, he spoke to me. Not with words of comfort or encouragement, but God put it to me to help someone else. I have since learned that's typical of God. It's not about me or us; our life needs to be about others. God told me to find Terry, the pastor of the church I had just left, and look after him as he was suffering terribly. I knew that God had spoken to me; I needed God to comfort me but all God wanted me to do was to comfort others. I managed to contact Terry by phone. It turned out that the other leaders had literally thrown him and his belongings out of the church. He had gone to stay at a hotel in Fort William, a town north of Glasgow. When I finally got him on the phone he told me he had suffered a nervous breakdown and had been contemplating suicide.

He apologised and repented for any part he had in the troubles that affected Tricia and me. We forgave him. He then travelled to Largs, the town we lived in, and I met him at a local hotel. He cried for six hours while he was with me, and I comforted him. Today he is remarried, happy and back in ministry. He is my best friend and biggest supporter in the world today. God is a restorer. None of the other leaders of that church continued in ministry for very long.

I was still broken though. Poor Tricia tried so hard to help me; she didn't know what to do. She would just hold me and try as best she could to comfort me. She was my tower of strength yet I needed to get back close to God; this was critical to me. 'What about me, God,' I would cry, 'I need comfort, peace and strength from you, too.' No answer came back, just silence – dreadful and dark silence. I knew that God was faithful. He had proved himself to me so many times but I had to remind myself every day that God is faithful.

I found some encouragement reading my old journals on how God had heard my prayers and helped me come through so much in the past. God was showing me that I needed to realise from past experiences with him that he would see me through. It slowly dawned on me that this experience had many lessons in it for me to learn and grow through. I just had to stick at it, believing that God would come through for me in the end.

I had no idea of what was about to happen in my life. Not in my wildest dreams could I have imagined what God was about to do.

Please Help Us, John!

One night during this time I received a call from a friend in Aberdeen. I had helped her daughter Sophie on a number of occasions. She was a lovely girl, but she was addicted to heroin, methadone and Valium. I had tried to help her detox on several occasions, managing to get her off heroin but struggling to get her off methadone and Valium. These are some of the hardest drugs to break free and withdraw from as the pain and withdrawals are often very frightening. Sophie tried so hard every time but just when she was about to get free she would panic and run away. Her mother told me that Sophie wanted to leave yet another rehabilitation centre; she had been in this rehab for just a short time. She told me that Sophie was frightened again and was demanding her medication from the staff. I listened carefully as she spoke, stopping now and then to control the tears she was once again shedding for the daughter she loved so much. I could hear her husband in the background speaking gently and comforting her. 'Please pray, John,' she pleaded. 'Please pray that Sophie will not leave again.' We all knew that this could be Sophie's last chance. If she didn't make it this time she would probably die, leaving behind her little boy and a broken family. I assured Sophie's mum and dad that I would pray. We spoke for a little longer before ending the conversation.

I turned to Tricia and related the situation to her. We both prayed, but once again I felt that my prayers were not getting through to God. I suggested to Tricia that she go to bed. 'I'll be up shortly,' I said. Tricia kissed me on the cheek before retiring.

I took my Bible out and got on my knees to read and pray. Bit by bit I pushed through in prayer for Sophie. I was very fond of her and I knew that deep down she desperately wanted to be free. I had been praying for about fifteen minutes on my own when suddenly something started to happen to me. The atmosphere in my living room began to change. I began to realise how self-centred I had been, how I had focused on myself, my hurt, my pain, my circumstance, my pity party. I was not the man of God I thought I had been. I began to realise how much I had let my circumstances bind me.

By this time I was lying face down on the carpet and pleading with God to forgive me for my sin of self-centredness and for wanting my own personal needs to be met. For the first time in months I began to hear God speak to me for my own sake. I was surprised and delighted to hear that still, small voice. The wonderful and amazing presence of God began to come into the room where I was praying. In my mind I saw Jesus on the cross. He had been accused of things he had never done. During Jesus' life all he had done was show love, heal and help people. Then during his greatest time of need he refused to become self-centred or feel sorry for himself. On the contrary, he began reaching out to help others. Many of his followers, including his close friends, had denied him or followed him from a distance. I saw how Jesus had paid the price for everything I had been through. He did not try to defend himself, vindicate himself or get attention for himself – even when everything earthly was robbed from him and his clothes were taken and shared amongst his accusers. No, instead he prayed, 'Father, forgive them for they know not what they do.'

'Wow!' I cried. In his time of greatest need he looked after those who were around him. I was blessed and surprised to realise that he loved everyone around him, even his accusers and murderers. He was still Lord of love as he hung on the cross. He had completely and totally forgiven all those who had ever sinned against him. I knew that I must do the same. Just before Jesus died he spoke to the thief on the other cross saying, 'Today you will be with me in paradise.' Then he told his disciples to look after Mary, his mother. Only when he had taken care of everyone close to him did he die for all mankind. He uttered his final words: 'Father, into your hands I commit my spirit.' This was it. I believe God was saying that he was looking for people who would forsake what they needed most, no matter what that was, and focus on caring for the needs of others.

I had always thought I put others first, but realised I had never put them first to this degree. I felt God gently touch me, saying to my heart that he wanted me to respond to hurt like he did; to come to a place in my mind and spirit where I would be completely dead to self. I knew instinctively that I could not do this on my own. It would take an action from God to do this work in me. I didn't feel release from my own pain, which I could still feel deep in my soul. It had become my constant but unwelcome companion. I knew now that Jesus wanted me to always look after others no matter what I was going through. I responded to Jesus in my heart saying, 'I will do it. I will do it, Jesus, but help me. I don't have the ability to do this in my own strength.'

The presence of God touched me, that small voice said, 'Learn from me for my yoke is easy, my burden is light.' Then I sensed God say, 'Start with Sophie.' I began to pray for her, long sobs began to come from me as I could see Jesus loving others through tears that mingled with blood from his crown of thorns put there by his accusers.

Words from one of my spiritual fathers, Mr Hugh Black, came to me. 'John,' he'd say, 'you are like a son to me; learn from me. You must learn to embrace darkness

41

without care for yourself, it is only then that you can come into true light. Squeeze every bit of life out of darkness. When life breaks you, John, stay broken, stay relying on God's power. When you come to the day when your power, personality or calling cannot hold you anymore, only then do you see true light.'

Earth's darkest day was when Jesus hung on the cross, yet it was only hours before the greatest light that the universe or eternity has ever witnessed was unveiled. Mr Black warned me that I would one day experience what he called 'the dark night of the soul': 'Come through it, John, push through, for life is at the far side.' Wow, it's happening, I realised. God was giving me treasure out of darkness. I was now beginning to have an experience in intercession and deep prayer. I knew that God was hearing my prayers for Sophie. In fact, it was like he was praying with me or even through me for her. The prayers were more than human; they had something of the divine in them.

Suddenly I felt exhausted, yet I believed the prayer for Sophie had been heard, all I had to do now was to wait for the answer. I have had only a few experiences in prayer like this but when they occurred I knew for certain that they were answered. I pulled myself to my feet. Looking at my watch I was amazed to see that an hour and a half had passed. Walking towards my bedroom I could feel something had changed in me. Some of my pain had eased; I knew God had done a work in me. 'Thank you so much, Jesus,' I said. 'Thank you for showing me light in my darkness.' I was delighted with the prayer time; I felt it marked a turnaround in my life. I was now, at last, definitely strengthened and more able to press on! Hallelujah! I whispered as I opened my bedroom door.

Chapter 4
For Heaven's Sake

It was dark in our room. I crept in without putting on the light. Trish was sleeping peacefully and I slipped into bed, like I did every night. However, tonight as I lay down to put my head on my pillow I felt the presence of God come upon me unexpectedly and powerfully. It was sudden, beautiful and without warning.

Instantly I was lifted out of my present reality and brought into another reality. I was shocked, a little frightened because I was now in a large room – a rectangle, about sixty-feet long and forty-feet wide. I instantly knew by revelation that I was here to meet with and talk to God. This knowledge was almost overwhelming. The room resembled a large waiting room that you would find in a bus or train station. There were many seats positioned along the middle of the room, a screen that looked a bit like a big plasma TV was down the far left-hand corner. The screen was placed about four-feet up on the wall; it was blank, there was nothing happening on it, yet I sensed it would have a part to play in whatever was going on with me.

'Where am I?' I wondered. 'What is this room?' As soon

as I thought these thoughts it dawned on me that I was in a waiting room to go into heaven. I heard a voice saying, 'Your life is being examined.' Knowledge came to me by revelation; as soon as I asked a question within myself the answer came. I didn't so much hear a voice; it was an inner, revelatory voice that spoke to me.

I knew for sure that at the far side of the right-hand wall I was standing beside, angels or some other heavenly be- ings were checking and searching through my life to see if I was worthy to get into heaven. Now I was not afraid at being in the room, but when I realised my life was being examined to see if I was worthy to go to heaven, I was completely terrified. Remember all the rumours, all the lies that had been told about me? I had felt a failure, un- worthy to serve God. The recent trauma had convinced me that I was just an ex-addict who had delusions about serv- ing God. I was looking for a job, any job to get by in life. Somehow, these feelings were present in my soul; I could feel what others had said about me. I had a real knowledge that I had been saved but somehow the words of others had completely knocked me to the point that I wasn't sure of anything anymore. The Bible tells us that there is life and death in the tongue – let us never forget that.

I looked down towards my feet. I noticed my knees shaking uncontrollably; nothing could stop them from shaking. I was terrified. Not the normal terror you get in frightening situations; no, this was a terror of God. Sins I had committed during my life came back to memory– not just big ones. What people would call minor sins were suddenly huge sins, and they would definitely keep me out of heaven and I knew I was in no way worthy to go there. I was lost, completely lost and without hope outside of God. Surely without accepting Christ and his sacrifice for sin I cannot ever go into heaven? God would never let the sin in me go into heaven, I knew that for sure. Thoughts and actions that I never considered to be sins were sinful to God – not just sinful but absolutely abhorrent. I knew that neither I nor anyone on the face of the earth is worthy to go to heaven on their own merit. That moment I knew for certain that I, along with all mankind, am totally dependent on God for salvation. The fear of God gripped me. I never had one thought of hell. The dreadful realisation that I may not be able to get into heaven was more frightening, eternally frightening, than any earthly fear or fright that can ever possess me again.

I questioned myself at this point, asking myself, 'Do I truly trust Christ and his blood to have washed away my sin? Am I a Christian?' These and other similar questions assaulted me with doubt and weak hope. Deep within myself I detected a trust in Christ and his blood; my complete trust in Christ and the finished work of the cross was much weaker than I had ever imagined it to be. I knew all my self-righteousness was as filthy rags before a holy God.

Suddenly a voice came from the direction of the big screen at the other end of the room. 'John Charles Edwards,' the voice boomed, 'come forward.' I was being called to go up to the screen. I instantly knew that I was going to be told whether I could go into heaven or not. I didn't know at this stage what was going to happen. I began the frightening walk towards the screen. Step by step, down past the chairs in the middle of the room.

Turning left at the end of the chairs I walked the last fifteen feet or so until I stood about four or five feet in front of the screen. I was holding my head down in shame, conscious of the sinful state of my life. I felt shame, awful and deep shame; surely I was wretched in God's sight. Then the voice spoke again. The words seemed to go through me, not just into my ears; it was more like I heard with my heart. All of me seemed to hear this voice. 'Lift your head,' the Voice said. Slowly, guiltily I lifted my head. I looked at the screen but could not make out the face on it. However, I knew that it was the face of God. The scripture came to me that no man can see the face of God and live.

'John Charles Edwards,' the voice boomed, 'your life has been examined and you have been found to be innocent because of the blood of Jesus Christ. Enter into rest.'

The realisation that I am justified by faith hit me like nothing had ever hit me in my life before. I was instantly filled with miraculous relief and a joy unspeakable; revelations of salvation flooded my whole being. I was completely loved and accepted by God, I was complete and without sin. My troubles on earth were not on my mind at all now, just an inexplicable joy at knowing that I qualified for heaven because of Jesus Christ's sacrifice. I didn't jump up and down or rejoice in an earthly way, I just stood there, relieved – relieved in a way that no human pen can describe.

Just then a noise to my right caught my attention. I turned my head to see an elderly man or angel was walking towards me. I don't know what or who he was, it didn't seem to matter at the time, but for simplicity sake we'll call him an angel. He looked like he was in his mid-to-late seventies. He was dressed in a high-ranking dark blue military uniform. Medals from battles fought and victories won hung on his chest. His face had a healthy ruddy tone, his hair was short, neat and white, very white, and his eyes blue like the bluest sky on the best day you ever saw.

I had no idea why he was walking towards me; I just stood and stared at him. I was not frightened, my mind and spirit were flowing with this experience. The sense of rest and assurance I had received from the clear knowledge that I was sin free and justified by faith was still over-whelming me. He walked around and behind me, until he was standing to the front and left side of my body. He was staring straight at me and then he said, 'John, look at me.' As I looked into his eyes more peace – a different peace – flooded into my whole being. Healing seemed to pour into my soul. Then he opened his mouth and uttered these amazing words: 'You have suffered much pain, haven't you, John?'

'Yes, I have,' I answered, thinking of the treatment I had had from my Christian brothers and friends.

Again he said, 'You have suffered much distress, John, haven't you?'

'Yes, I have,' I answered again.

Finally he said, 'You have suffered much hurt, haven't you, John?'

'I have,' I answered. I looked at him, expecting him to say something.

At last he said, 'John, you will never suffer like that again! Come with me.' He then took hold of my left arm just at the elbow. He turned me round and walked with me towards the right-hand wall. I was not aware if the face on the screen was still there as I was completely taken up by this conversation with the elderly man or angel. He led me for three or four steps in the direction of the wall on my right. Suddenly and unexpectedly we left the room through an invisible wall. I couldn't see this wall, I know that it was spiritual, though, for I let out a little scream of fear as we passed through it. My flesh was shocked by the passing from the room to this next place; we had entered the lower parts of heaven.

I was filled instantly with the pure presence of God. I exclaimed out loud, 'In his presence is fullness of joy.' I was not saying it to the angel, I was saying it to myself. The angel was still holding my left arm at my elbow. This part of heaven was not spectacular to look at. It was not dark, yet the distance beyond us was black like velvet, there were lights everywhere, they could have been stars, or planets, or just lights, and I didn't pay them particular attention. I was too caught up with the presence of God. I could see no beginning or end to it. There was a sense of eternity here, also a sense of everlasting but accessible distance. Here on earth we know that space is never ending, and we know we can never travel to its end. Here in heaven the distance could be travelled; why I knew it I don't know, I just knew it. Lights like stars were everywhere, like I was in space, yet it was heaven.

We seemed to be hovering – I was not aware of gravitational pull in any direction, nor did I sense weightlessness. I just felt normal in my body besides being filled with God's presence. The angel turned to go behind me, then taking hold of my right arm just above my wrist he pointed upwards and said, 'Look.'

I looked up. High up in heaven there was a being moving through heaven's space down towards us. It was a younger being, another angel or whatever they were. His clothing was not special nor spectacular. I didn't notice any wings, nor did I pay any attention to or memorise how he was dressed. He travelled down towards me and when he reached me he took hold of my left arm at the same place where the old angel had previously held me and said that I must come with him. 'I have something to show you, John,' he said. I was not surprised that he knew my name.

The two angels took off flying, holding me by the arms between them. I don't know if flying is the right term, we just seemed to move at a speed that cannot be measured in miles per hour. The further we went the stronger the presence of God became, to the extent that I thought I would lose consciousness. It was then that I realised I was probably still in my earthly body. I knew if the presence of God got any stronger it was likely my body would not be able to stand the purity of God's presence; I felt it could die. Perhaps this is what the apostle Paul meant when he wrote in 2 Corinthians 12:2, 'I know a man in Christ who fourteen years ago was caught up to the third heaven. Whether it was in the body or out of the body I do not know – God knows.'

Was this now what I was experiencing?

With that the young angel let go of me and we all stopped. The old angel stayed at my right-hand side while the young one went about five feet ahead and to our right; he was facing me. The older angel told me to pay attention to what the younger angel was doing. I turned my attention towards him. He was looking out to his right and my left, and suddenly he moved his right arm in a sweeping gesture from his left to his right. I was amazed as an entire area opened up and revealed a huge rectangle that was way below us. On it were what looked like roads or paths. 'What is it?' I asked. The old angel replied, 'This is the earth and on it you see the paths of life.'

I looked closer, the earth I saw before me was nothing like we see on television or in pictures or atlases. It was rectangular, flat, and on it were lots of paths – not hundreds but lots – I didn't try to count them, it didn't seem necessary. I just knew somehow that I was about to be shown something significant. I looked intently at the paths of life. I began to make out many people walking on the paths. Some of the paths were straight and narrow, while all the others were broad and wide. I knew that the narrow paths were where Christians walked on earth; the wide paths were where non-Christians walked.

Suddenly I heard a voice speaking, a separate voice from the two angels, and the voice began to speak about seasons. 'There is a time for everything, and everything on earth has its special season. There is a time to be born and a time to die, there is time to plant and time to pull up plants, there is a time to cry and a time to laugh.' So some, but not all of the scriptures from the third chapter of Ecclesiastes were quoted. As he spoke I could see the beginning of everyone's life on earth, their life began at the start of each path of life and they ended at the end of the path. Each one was according to God's perfect will, so the voice quoted the verses until I could see at the end of every path the death that was destined for each and every person on earth. The Christians were dropping off the end of their paths and going straight to eternity and into God's presence. The non-Christians death was sealed in a huge glass-type vessel; in the middle of each of these glass-type vessels there was a false god – it looked exactly like a Buddha. In the belly of each Buddha was what looked like a film playing of the death assigned to each non-Christian. One had a storm with a shipwreck in it. Another had a shark in the belly and it was eating a man. They died not knowing Christ, and went straight into hell. This was not God's will. I was horrified. 'Why won't someone tell them?' I screamed. 'What's wrong with the Christians?'

I looked back down the paths of life at all the Christians. They were dressed in drab clothes and they were walking slowly with their heads hanging, eyes focused on the ground in front of them. I looked back down towards the end of the paths. The non-Christians were still falling into a lost eternity. 'Why? Why won't someone tell them?' I cried again. I was sobbing now. I pleaded with loud sobbing cries for God to intervene. I looked at the Christians again. They were depressed, but more than that, they were only concerned with their own lives and were under the oppression of the devil.

The older angel was still holding me by my right arm. He got my attention by squeezing it hard, 'Look, John,' he said. With that the younger angel went at incredible speed towards the paths on earth. I could see him clearly as he flew down. He went to the very beginning of the path furthest from me and put his two hands on the start of it. It was a straight and narrow path; Christians were on it. Thinking back now it is strange: the angel didn't seem to get any bigger and the paths came no closer yet I could see what was going on very clearly. With no effort the angel picked up the entire path, from birth to death. I could see three dimensions of the path as he lifted it up. He flew up with it and when he had reached a good height he tipped the end of the path down until it touched a wide and broad path. This was a moment of divine appointment for the non-Christian on it. I looked at the Christians on the path that was being used to reach the non-Christians. None of them had changed the way they were walking, they were completely unaware and uncaring that God was about to use them. They still walked with their heads down, oppressed and sad looking, when in reality they should have been rejoicing because they were on their way to heaven.

The paths touched and, as they did so, a brown wooden cross unexpectedly shot straight down from heaven. No one was on it. The cross landed and stuck like a dagger at exactly the spot where the two paths met. Instantly the wide path turned into a narrow path and the Buddha and glass vial-type container with their death in it vanished from the end of the path. The people's eternal destiny had changed. I had stopped weeping. I looked in wonder as I realised how privileged the people were to be involved in the miracle of salvation. Yet they still walked not caring about their fellow man; they still only cared about themselves, their path and their circumstances. They were alive to themselves and to their situations, but not to God's plans or purpose.

I then began to be pulled out of my visit to heaven. As I was being drawn out I seemed to go upwards, to the left and away from the grip of the older angel. He didn't say goodbye; I knew somehow that I would meet him again someday. Suddenly a voice from my right, high up in heaven, spoke. It was a voice that sounded like a thunderous waterfall – I believe it was the voice of God. The voice went right through me in such a way that it felt like it added something to me. I felt weighted but gifted by it, like it became part of me. The voice said, 'John Charles Edwards, take the gospel to the lost, and take the cross to my people.' And again, 'John Charles Edwards, take the gospel to the lost and take the cross to my people.' The voice continued to repeat this command and, as it did so, I could see thousands of crosses fall on the paths of life. Holy mayhem broke loose on the earth, wide paths were becoming straight everywhere, Buddhas were vanishing, eternal destinies were being changed.

Then, suddenly, I came back to earthly reality on my bed. I sat up, the whole room was filled with the glory of God; the incredible presence and glory of God was still with me. I sat in it for a while, basking, awed by the privilege of what had just happened. Slowly, I came to my senses. I looked over at Tricia who was sleeping soundly by my side. I nudged her, she woke up and, looking at me through sleepy eyes, she could see that something had happened to me. Sitting up she stared at me and said, 'What's happened to you?' I excitedly told her the entire story. She said she was amazed at the difference in me, I reminded her of Moses when he came down from the mountain, the glory shining from him. I looked at our bedroom clock; nearly three hours had passed. I had been in heaven for three hours. I had such a wonderful knowledge of justification by faith alone. I felt clean, like nothing anyone could say to me would ever deeply upset or affect me again. I knew without a shadow of doubt that I had been in heaven and that I had been commissioned by God himself to preach the gospel.

I have total confidence in God's calling now and have never doubted again the call God has on my life. Of course I could not sleep after that. I got up and wrote down the entire experience in my journal in our living room.

Later that morning, about nine thirty, the phone rang. It was Sophie's mum. 'John,' she said excitedly, 'Sophie has had a miracle! She got up in the middle of the night and demanded her medication. She trampled every pill she had into dust and has been completely set free!' I told Sophie's mum the story of what had happened to me and together we rejoiced at the amazing power of God.

Today Sophie is married and lives in Perth, Scotland. She has a lovely new baby and is a happy, settled mum ... Now that is what I call a divine appointment.

Chapter 5
Godly Provision

Not surprisingly, life took on a new perspective after this experience. I had my vision to serve God back, accompanied by the knowledge that I was called by God to bring the gospel to the world. Unfortunately, this didn't mean that miraculous money or pennies from heaven just came down and provided me with enough finance to do what God wanted me to do. No, God expects us to live by faith, for without faith we cannot please God. Tricia and I were still a little bruised and hurting after the trauma of the church split. We were left without a wage and things were sometimes difficult. With no job, no visible source of income and no work on the way, we struggled. These were difficult times for us. Christmas was fast approaching, and there were four kids to buy presents for. You may remember from my book *Walking Free* that I had learned lessons in how to live by faith.

Before I was married I had run a rehab without receiving any personal income, trusting God for many things, and always he proved himself faithful to me. Now, however, things were different. I remember when we first got married, the shock it was to me to have to provide not just for myself but for six of us. I had been a single man for forty-two years, never having lived with someone else. But when I got married there were six of us overnight. Ha! We Irish men work quickly. You have no idea how this changed my life.

For example, when I was single I used to go down to the supermarket to get my weekly shopping. I would get my little supermarket hand-held shopping basket and within ten or fifteen minutes I would have my shopping done. A pack of fish-fingers, a couple of pork or lamb chops, some mince or stewing steak, lambs' liver, a few cans of beans, some cereal and, of course, toilet rolls. A pack of four toilet rolls did me for quite a long time. My father had always taught us in Ireland to be economical with how many toilet rolls we used. I can remember him roaring at us, 'Them toilet rolls are going too quickly. You kids are using too much. Use less! Do you think they grow on trees or something?' I remember thinking to myself that in fact they do grow on trees: paper is made from wood. I didn't have the nerve to remind him though. Dad was one of those guys that used to check the immersion heater in our house and if it was too high he would turn it down, meaning the water was always lukewarm. When he wasn't watching, my sisters would put it back up again, much to my father's annoyance. I am not like my dad in this way, at least I didn't think I was, but I will never forget my first trip to the supermarket with Tricia. We were married only a matter of weeks, in fact we had just come back from our honeymoon and normal life as a happily married couple was beginning.

On arrival at the supermarket Tricia picked the biggest shopping trolley she could find, which in itself surprised me. I mean this trolley was huge! Never having used one of those trolleys in my entire life I was quite unprepared for what was about to happen. Looking back now I don't know what I was thinking about. I guess like many newly married guys I still had the mentality of a single man in some ways. Anyway, Tricia took this trolley and off we went through the aisles of the supermarket. She put in something from just about every shelf. I had never noticed the signs that said 'buy one get one free' or 'two for the price of one'. Single men don't seem to notice these offers. Shopping is like going on a mission for us: we go into the shop, zoom around picking up exactly what we need; within minutes we're done and out of there.

When the shopping trolley was full, and I mean full, Tricia put the icing on the cake by adding two six-packs of toilet rolls on top. I mean this was a balancing act that belonged in a circus; even God couldn't have got more into that trolley! Oh! By the way, the toilet rolls were, 'buy one get one free'. I could not believe it: that many toilet rolls would have done me for six months. Seriously! We nearly had an argument over it. I could hear the echo of my father's voice coming through me.

'Your kids are going to have to learn to use less toilet roll, Tricia. Two six-pack rolls is uneconomical and ridiculous. You'll have to have a word with them.' Tricia's big beautiful eyes looked at me with surprise. She wasn't expecting this from me. Then she laughed and laughed. I got quite upset and ended up walking out of the shop. I got in our car and sulked, telling myself and God that I would have to teach this family a thing or two about shopping. I know, I thought, I'll teach Tricia how to shop while being led by the Holy Spirit. I'll tell her to go into the shop and to ask God what he really wanted her to get this week. She could begin by getting a smaller shopping trolley to start with. Later, when I made this suggestion it was met by further laughter from Tricia. After a few weeks I eventually saw the funny side and laughed with her. You will be happy to know that I have been set free from this conditioning and now I use as much toilet roll as I like without feeling guilty about it.

I had to have the last laugh though. At Christmas I bought all the kids a roll of the softest, most expensive toilet roll I could find and wrapped them beautifully and put them under the Christmas tree. That got a laugh and they still chide me for it today.

Christmas Crackers

I normally went home to Ireland for Christmas and New Year to be with my family, but now I had a ready-made family of my own and was looking forward to our first happy Christmas together. This posed more problems of provision for me. How would I manage to look after all the extra needs that arose for my own family?

This was a testing time for us. Shortly before Christmas my car broke down and was in the garage being repaired. I didn't have the finance to pay for it and was praying hard for God to provide. One of my friends was going to Africa on a mission and she kindly offered me a loan of her little Citroen until she came back on Christmas Eve. Unfortunately, the exhaust fell off her car one day while I was driving to Glasgow. I had to put her car in the garage too. The mechanic told me that he could not get the exhaust for the car until after Christmas and unfortunately my friend needed it by Christmas Eve.

My stepson Kevin also needed a job, and Tricia and I needed to buy all the kids' presents. I was getting worried. We ran out of money on the same day and we needed food in the house. I knew that God is faithful. He had never let me down in the past and I was confident he would meet our needs again. But I also knew from past experiences that serious prayer was needed.

Don't forget we were still working with the addicts. One family in particular needed help. They left the rehab they were in because the police had come to it and locked the father up for a minor offence he had committed several months before. This threw the whole family up in the air. They left the rehab and arrived home in Ayrshire the next day, all five of them. The local church wouldn't help them as they felt it was unwise to leave rehab and the family would have to suffer the consequences of their wrong choice. Oh how often I have seen that happen, so once again I saw it as my responsibility to look after them. I get so angry with the courts when they do this type of thing.

I remember when I was working with a fourteen-year-old heroin addict, the powers-that-be claimed he was too young to go to rehab, and that he would have to wait till he was sixteen – for health and safety reasons, of course. While he was waiting for these two years I continued working with him. He committed some minor crimes to get money to feed his drug habit during this time. I finally got him into rehab when he turned sixteen. He was there for just a few weeks when the police came and arrested him for one of the minor crimes he'd committed while he was waiting to be old enough to go to rehab. He got so discouraged he went away from me and I am afraid I have not seen him in years. AAAGGHHH! I pray for him and trust that what God began in him, he will complete. Just recently another guy I'd been working with for several years was, at long last, meant to go to rehab. However, he was found dead the week before. I spoke at his funeral.

Anyway, I digress ... that was a little peek into my world today. Let's go back to my first Christmas.

I saw it as my responsibility to look after the family who

had left rehab and I needed miracles. There was no possible way for me to get the money I would need to do all my shopping and meet the needs for my family and the addicts. I knew it would take a move of God to provide for all we needed. I decided to go to my special prayer place: a hill at the back of Largs, the little town where we lived in Ayrshire. The hill is about a thousand feet above the town and from there I could see the entire area we lived in. There was a reason I had picked this spot for battling in prayer. Going up here reminded me that we are seated in heavenly places in Christ; far above all powers, all principalities, over the works of the devil, over debt, over sickness, over doubt and worry, over everything. I had fought and won many a battle in prayer as a single man from this particular pulpit in the sky. Now, as a married man, I needed to pray and see the Word of God come to pass for my entire family.

Before I went up I went around the house and picked up every penny I could find, a penny here, fifty pence there; the total came to just under £5. I bought a couple of small items from our local shop that we needed urgently which left me with £3.

I told Tricia what I was going to do and then went round the back of our house and climbed to my 1,000-foot high prayer closet. My friend Shay Phelan was staying with us during this time and he came along with me. Shay and I positioned ourselves in a spot where we could look down on our house and town. I took out my little Bible and opened it at Philippians 4:19 which says: 'My God will meet all your needs according to the riches of his glory in Christ Jesus.' Then I put my hand in my pocket and took out the £3 I had left – this was all I had to my name. I looked at it first and then looked down at my house 1,000 feet below, knowing that this miserly £3 was all I had to meet my family's needs for Christmas. Many people in a situation like this would get discouraged and depressed but I had learned over the years that God is faithful. I also know that God answers prayer.

I looked at the £3 in my hand, and then looked again at the house. I looked down at the bank at the other end of the town; I had been receiving letters from them telling me I had exceeded my overdraft limit. Then I looked down at the garage where I had two cars parked that needed fixing. Taking the £3 in my right hand I shouted into the air above Largs, 'God, I cannot live according to what I have in my pocket. I refuse to live by the report the bank and my circumstances are dictating to me. I choose to live according to your glorious riches in Christ Jesus.' With that I took the £3 in my hand and flung them as far down the hill as I could, far enough so as I knew I couldn't find them if I tried. Shay was looking at me a little strangely. I think he thought I was losing the plot. With that I roared at the top of my voice, 'God, I trust you to provide for me and my family for this Christmas.' I repeated Philippians 4:19 over and over, 'My God will meet all your needs according to his riches in glory by Christ Jesus.' As I did so the wind began to blow stronger and stronger. When I had first climbed up there was hardly any wind at all. I kept this up for about thirty minutes or so, until Shay and I were literally leaning into the wind with our arms outstretched. I looked at my house and declared that Kevin would get a job, that the kids would be provided with presents and that Tricia and I would be able to celebrate God's faithfulness over Christmas.

I then turned my gaze to the bank and declared that I would only believe the report of the Lord. That in him I was not overdrawn on his account ... and never would be. Looking down at the garage I declared that the cars would be fixed and my friend would have her car back by Christmas

Eve. I then turned my attention to pray for the needs of the family who had just left rehab. 'God,' I cried, 'you know their needs: those kids need a Christmas, they need to see your faithfulness in the midst of their lives.' I declared over that family that God would supply all their needs.

I kept this up for another fifteen or twenty minutes, until I believed and felt in my heart that God had heard my prayer. I then climbed down from my position in victory, expectant for answered prayer.

Tricia was waiting for us when we returned and she had a big smile on her face that told me something had happened already. 'John, you'll never believe what has happened while you were up praying.' I couldn't wait so I urged her to tell me immediately. She continued, 'We just got a phone call and someone has put a thousand pounds into our bank account. Not only that, but Kevin also got a call telling him that he got that job he was interviewed for last week.' But that wasn't all, there were still more answers to prayer.

The garage owner had phoned and declared that there must be a Santa, because he found an exhaust in the corner of his garage that fits a Citroen. He said he didn't know it was there and couldn't understand how he hadn't seen it before. The garage owner told Tricia the car would be ready for the next day. Oh, how we rejoiced! God had answered our prayers immediately. He is faithful, especially when we are putting others first – then it seems he answers prayers in double time.

Unfortunately not many are prepared to go the extra mile in prayer. Allowing themselves to get depressed or dejected, they hold a pity party instead of pressing through in prayer and believing that nothing is impossible with God. I heard someone saying once, 'If you want to experience the impossible you must be able to see the invisible.'

That is so true. The next morning someone else put more money into our account and others blessed us during the week. We had enough to get all the kids good presents. We feasted on a full Christmas dinner with all the trimmings, too. The cars were mended in time for Christmas, Kevin had a job, and the addicted family we were working with enjoyed celebrating Christmas day in a new rented house with presents for everyone. God is good, God is faithful.

Tricia and I didn't have enough money for presents for each other. We did, however, have £40 left to pay the electricity bill so Tricia suggested we used it to buy each other a present. We would keep the receipts and return them just after Christmas, this way we would still have the fun of opening a present on Christmas morning. We bought each other lovely presents that we could open together with the kids. They had no idea of the struggle we had just days before; we wanted to spare them from the worry. That first Christmas as a married couple was wonderful. We opened our presents together, including the kids' toilet rolls. Tricia and I took photos in our new dressing gowns that we bought. Then as soon as the shops were open after Christmas we took them back with the receipts for a refund so we could pay the electricity bill.

Such are the lessons of faith, but we know that our God will supply all our needs according to his glorious riches in Christ Jesus. I hope that you, too, will be prepared to go to your prayer closet when the going gets tough.

Chapter 6
Take Up Your Cross, John

Not long before I had my visit to heaven, I had been praying and walking through different countries. It's hard to imagine now how I managed to fit all this in. Let me tell you how I began to do this amazing ministry.

In 1993 I was reading through the book of Genesis in the Bible. I came to chapter 13 verse 17 which says, 'Go, walk through the length and breadth of the land, for I am giving it to you.' While I was reading, this scripture verse really caught my attention. I genuinely believed God was asking me to do it. I immediately said I would. So began my walking ministry. I decided to call this ministry Walking Free. I thought of it one day when I was in a car with John Macey who was at that time the national director of Teen Challenge Britain. I undertook to walk in Ireland. I had no car, no money but I had two strong legs and I was both willing and fit.

My first ever experience of prayer walking was actually back in 1989 – I walked around the Cathedral in Galway on the west coast of Ireland, praying for God to touch Galway city. It was only in 1993 my serious walks started, together with some friends, which included former terrorists from the Ulster Volunteer Force (UVF). We walked from Belfast to Dublin, beginning in a church called The Stadium. This church was pastored by Jack McKey and was situated on the infamous Shankill Road in Belfast. We walked, prayed and preached our way through the nationalist and loyalist areas of Belfast and Northern Ireland. We stopped at the border and worshipped God while we prayed that God would unite Ireland and take the borders down and bring a revival. Today the borders are down and peace reigns in Ireland. I do a lot of work now in the north of Ireland. Just recently God gave us a breakthrough on the Falls Road in west Belfast. My friends from Falls Road are working with my church there, Life Church Belfast, and we plan to start a prayer meeting soon for the lovely folk of west Belfast.

During the walks we averaged at least twenty-five miles a day and experienced God's answer to many prayers on the way. Indeed I believe miracles have happened as a direct result of this walk. I then walked through the length and breadth of Wales, praying for revival. This was both a prayer and fundraising walk. We raised nearly £8,000 during the Welsh walk. That was the first money that Teen Challenge raised towards buying land in Bombay (now Mumbai) in India. They now boast a full-blown rehabilitation village just outside Mumbai. What a privilege to have been part of such a great exploit.

I used the name Walking Free for the first time during this walk. We had T-shirts printed with a pair of trainers emblazoned on them, with the name 'Walking Free' printed over them in red. I went into schools to speak to hundreds of young people about the dangers of drug abuse. The kids from these schools in South Wales undertook their own local sponsored walks, declaring as they went that they were

Walking Free from life-controlling problems. These kids managed to raise over £2,000 towards the rehabilitation of addicts with Teen Challenge. I believe many of them were deeply influenced by our visits and their sponsored walks. I often think of them and pray that they are all doing well and have managed to stay drug free.

My body ached during these walks: the going can be tortuous with blisters, shin splints, and both biting cold and sweltering heat. Walking on the roads is a skill that can only be learned by doing it. Knowing how to walk safely, not being a danger to passing cars and ensuring your own safety are skills that few would be willing to learn.

My next long walk was through the length and breadth of Ireland, beginning in Mizzen Head in the very south of Ireland. We again walked an average of twenty-five miles a day, five or six days a week. We so enjoyed walking and praying through the length and breadth of my lovely Ireland. We prayed that God would heal our land and set the addict free. My friend and fellow minister Shay Phelan walked with me while Liam Joyce, who was then director of Teen Challenge Ireland, drove our caravan. We took another friend along for part of the trip; his name was Tony, and he was a recovering alcoholic. Tony had been a bank robber at one time. He was a real character. Once he and a friend dressed as priests; Tony sat in a wheelchair with a blanket over his legs, but under the blanket was a sawn-off shotgun. When they entered the bank Tony took out the gun and held everyone at gunpoint while they emptied the teller's tills of money. They got caught, though, and Tony spent a long time in prison for his unsuccessful exploits. Tony gave his life to Christ and came to our church in Dublin for a season. I got him a flat right across the corridor from my own place and he did very well for a while.

Unfortunately he had a slip and, while visiting his hometown of Limerick, some old enemies dragged him down a back alley and beat him to death. I believe Tony is in heaven now as he accepted Christ as his Saviour. This is why, when I train outreach teams, I urge them to always endeavour to lead people to Christ and pray that they become saved. Oh the prayers that went up for the addicts during that walk. The presence of God was so real to us during that time.

A Call to the World

One day we were walking just outside Athlone, a large town in the middle of Ireland. It was coming towards the end of the day's walk. Shay was a bit ahead of me; he was walking a bit quicker than me that day. Usually I would be way ahead of him, but today for some reason I was lagging behind. We both had our paces, sometimes I would run, but Shay would always walk. This day I was praying while walking on the side of a narrow country road, and then suddenly everything went quiet. The sort of peace and stillness that comes just before you realise God is going to speak to you. I stopped in my tracks. No cars were coming; it was just me, the beautiful Irish countryside and God. The sun was shining, I remember it clearly; the weather was warm but not too warm. I was feeling good but looking forward to finishing my walk for the day. It was then I heard that still small voice speaking: 'John, will you go around the world preaching the gospel?' This was not a statement but a question: was I willing to do it? God is so gracious when he asks, always the gentleman, not forcing his will on us but rather looking for our willingness. I had learned to listen for his voice. This was one of those moments and I fell to my knees at the side of the road. 'Yes, Lord,' I answered, 'I will walk the whole way round the world if you want. I will do anything to preach your gospel.'

Then, just as suddenly as I had felt the Holy presence of God come to me on the road, it left. I was now on my own, still on my knees. I stood up, not sure what to do. Suddenly a fear began to grip me, like the enemy was trying to rob the moment from me. I imagined myself walking through deserts, cities in foreign countries; fears of being attacked and killed invaded my thoughts. I imagined mountain lions creeping up on me, radical Muslims trying to kill me, or being knocked down by a car. I pulled myself together and continued to walk at my four-miles-an-hour pace.

When I reached Shay and Liam in the caravan I shared with them what had happened on the road. 'God wants me to go round the world preaching the gospel,' I said. 'I'm afraid to do it, yet I said that I would do it.' I asked them to pray that God would confirm to me that he really wanted me to do it. We then drove to the house we were staying at that night. My friends Ken and Anne Ashworth were putting us up in their lovely home. They are American missionaries who felt the call to minister in Ireland. They own a lovely house on the shores of beautiful Lough Rea on the river Shannon. They gave us a huge welcome and settled us in. Anne ran a bath for me. 'Go on and jump in the bath before your dinner, John,' she said.

I headed for the bathroom. 'Hey John,' Ken shouted after me, 'I have a surprise for you when you've finished your bath.'

'Right, thanks Ken,' I answered.

After my bath I came down. Anne had made a huge dinner of spaghetti bolognese which was on the table, piping hot and ready for us to eat. 'Here, boys, lots of carbohydrates in this meal for your energy, it will keep you going for another day of your walk.' Ken was over in the corner of the kitchen fiddling with the TV. 'John, I want to show you a video while we're eating dinner. God put it on my heart to show it to you. This is the surprise!'

We sat down, said grace and got stuck into our meal. We were all ravenous with hunger. Ken put the video on: 'Here, guys, watch this,' Ken said as we tucked into Anne's delicious bolognese. I could hardly believe my eyes when the video started. It was the story of a guy called Arthur Blessitt who carries a cross around the world preaching the gospel. This video was about how God had protected him as he walked through some pretty dangerous countries. He had escaped from firing squads, been rescued after being kidnapped, gone through deserts unharmed by animals or hot sun. Every fear and danger I had imagined just hours before vanished as I saw God confirm his call on me to go round the world as he led me. Shay and Liam looked at me with amazement on their faces. God had confirmed to us his will. (In 2011 I had the privilege of having dinner with Arthur Blessitt and his family, and I carried my cross with him through west Belfast.)

From that moment on my destiny changed. Straight after I finished that walk I began to plan other walks. Next I walked through the length and breadth of Britain. On this walk I saw many become Christians. My prayer focus was once again on the addict. I made a 5-foot-long syringe out of the cardboard inside of a rolled-up carpet, putting a long white plastic 2-inch diameter pipe through the middle. I put red candle wax to resemble blood and angled the tip to look like the top of the needle. It looked fabulous and was sure to get attention as I walked. I cut a little door in the cardboard barrel of the syringe to put lots of prayer request in for addicts and their families. Then off I went, together with Shay and my great friend Gordon McRobbie from Scotland. I prayed that God would give me buildings for rehabs as I went. What a fabulous trip that was. Walking again between 25 and 55 miles a day we completed the walk successfully. We even stayed at the Queen's Balmoral estate, guests of her minister Reverend Bob Sloan.

We had a very funny situation at Balmoral. It had been raining that day and the visibility was not great, so for shelter and safety I wore my bright pink rain cape. I also had a blue baseball cap on under the pink hood. I must have looked a sight, many cars honked their horns and folk waved their hands out of car windows as they whizzed past us.

On my arrival outside the Balmoral estate we noticed that the Queen's flag was raised which meant that she was in residence at the castle. There is a little chapel just outside the Balmoral estate called Crathie Kirk. This quaint little chapel is where the Queen's minister takes services and also where the Royal Family attends church during their stays at Balmoral. I was way ahead of Shay again so while I waited I decided to walk up to the chapel to pray for the Queen and her family. So, up the winding path towards the chapel I walked and once I was outside I began to pray out loud for the Royal Family.

Now just picture this for a moment: there was me, a little Irishman dressed the way I was and praying that God would save the Queen and her family. While I was praying at the top of my voice I noticed out of the corner of my eye a Land Rover go by on the road outside the chapel – it was the Queen's police. They looked up at me standing resplendent in my pink cape and blue baseball cap with a large homemade syringe on my shoulder. They drove up and around the chapel and within five minutes they appeared at the bottom of the winding path, the same path I had walked up earlier. I quickly finished praying, straightened my pink cape in a feeble effort to look normal, and then I walked down towards where the police Land Rover was parked. Gordon had arrived by this time, too, and he was looking a little nervous. I must admit I was enjoying the moment. I thought to myself that the police must think I'm a complete nut.

'Who are you and what on earth are you doing?' the police asked me. They were out of the Land Rover now. 'My name is John Edwards and I'm doing a prayer walk through the length of Britain,' I answered.

They looked at the syringe on my shoulder and asked me, 'What in God's name is that for?'

I had trouble keeping a smile off my face as I explained to them the significance of the 5-foot-long syringe. The police said that I was a bit suspicious-looking and that they would like me to move on. I don't think my Irish accent did anything to help the situation! I took a deep breath before telling them that I could not move on as I was staying at Balmoral that night.

Well, when I said that they'd had enough. 'Sir, I'm sorry but you will have to move on right now.' I could see things from their perspective and understood their concern. I couldn't wait till they actually realised that I really was staying at Balmoral with the Queen's minister. Shay had caught up by this time and he joined in with us all. I told the police that I had been in touch with Her Majesty Queen Elizabeth's minister Reverend Bob Sloan, and that I had his personal phone number. The look on their faces was priceless. Oh my word! I was enjoying this so much; anyone who has ever been in trouble with the police will tell you that it's great fun to be stopped by them when you absolutely know you have done nothing wrong. I gave them the phone number and they phoned Reverend Bob. 'Reverend,' the police officer said, 'I have an Irishman here with me; I found him praying outside Crathie Kirk. He said that he is staying with you tonight with his two friends. Says he's walking the length of Britain. Do you know anything about this man?'

Oh, I was biting my lip trying to keep a straight face, it was brilliant. I am sure God has a sense of humour and I bet he was enjoying it just as much as I was. I could hear Bob Sloan laughing on the other end of the policeman's phone. 'Yes, he is staying with me tonight with his two friends; can you send them over please?'

The policeman wasn't too happy with it and he gruffly told me to make my way over to the gate of Balmoral where Reverend Bob would let us in. Shay, Gordon and I climbed into our car with the caravan on the back and drove through the gates of Balmoral where we were granted entry. We laughed so much it hurt. God does get us into the most unusual situations. Oh, I pray I get in more situations like that. Come on, God, let's have more fun together. This is part of what a personal relationship with God is about.

We had a great night with the Queen's minister and his wife, and we signed the visitors' book a couple of pages past where there was a double page signature of Queen Elizabeth. I asked the Reverend that night if the Queen was a Believer. 'I cannot answer that for you, John, but she does sit very comfortably under the gospel of Jesus Christ,' he answered. You can interpret that for yourself but I got the impression that she may be. There's enough prayer going up for her with millions singing 'God save our Queen' so the chances are good of her being a real Believer.

Perseverance

When I do my walks I have to be completely focused as the energy I use up on a daily basis is massive. Every day I walk the equivalent of a marathon, five or six days a week. Before I set off I study both the start and finish lines of the walk. Just before this particular walk I visited Lands End, where there is a finish line actually painted on the road. I memorised this and focused myself so much that I knew I would not stop until I crossed that line. I had planned to finish on Friday 6 November 1998. I planned to finish by four o'clock in the afternoon as I wanted to finish in good daylight so I could enjoy the moment all the more. That was my focus and I was absolutely determined to finish on time.

I managed to keep to my schedule all through the country until I crossed the border of Cornwall. I was all set to finish on time but on the Tuesday before the end of the walk I fell ill; so ill that I had to go to hospital for treatment. I had caught a stomach bug and couldn't even keep water down. The doctor in the hospital told me that I should not walk any further as I was too ill. They discharged me and I spent the day in bed in our caravan, too weak to walk or even eat. That meant I lost a day's mileage and was now a day behind. The next morning I felt a little better but still could not eat anything except a quarter bowl of breakfast cereal. Gordon and Shay tried to persuade me to stay in bed another day but I insisted on stepping out in faith, believing that God would give me the strength to finish the walk. Gordon reluctantly drove me back to the spot I finished at on the Monday evening. I got out of the car, stood on the spot and asked God for the strength to walk for the day. I walked all day without eating anything, only drinking a little water. I had diarrhoea and needed to stop many times but I kept going throughout that Wednesday and didn't finish till I had walked fifty-four miles. It was dark when I finished but I was almost back on schedule.

The next day Tricia and Amanda arrived to join us for

the final walk in. Then, on the final day, I walked forty miles and crossed the finish line at ten minutes to four. I thanked God I had done it, finishing on time. My phone rang as I crossed the finish line; it was an addict looking for help.

Chapter 7
Miracle on Orkney

During the British walk I felt that I should begin carrying a wooden cross, to draw attention to Christ. I had carried the syringe a long way and felt it was time to change the focus of my walks. The prayers I had carried for the addict were no longer burdening me so much; I began to have a burden for everyone. I wanted everyone on earth to hear the gospel and have a relationship with God. I couldn't understand why so many people were not interested in hearing about salvation or heaven. Why are people not interested in where they go when they die? If we emigrate to a foreign country or even if we go on holiday, we research the country we are heading for, we check out the job scene, what the weather is going to be like. We pick a reputable airline to ensure safe passage to our destination and we make sure the hotel or house we're staying in is up to standard. No one would pick a horrible place to go to on their holiday, and no one is going to emigrate to a country that they know they wouldn't like to live in. So why do people not research what happens when they die or what heaven is like?

The answer is that they are blinded to it. The Bible tells us in 2 Corinthians 4:4:

'The god of this age [Satan] has blinded the minds of unbelievers, so that they cannot see the light of the gospel that displays the glory of Christ, who is the image of God.'

This would be my life mission: to preach the gospel on the streets of the world, using whatever means I could to do so. The cross would be the ideal tool to draw people's attention to Christ. It's a bit hard to hide the fact you're a Christian when you have an eleven-foot wooden cross over your shoulder. That was it; from now on I would carry the cross. My mind was made up.

On completion of the British walk a friend made me an eleven-foot cross with a twelve-inch-diameter wheel on the end. I did not know if I would be able to carry this very far so I picked a short walk to test it.

Let me tell you that carrying an eleven-foot cross is not only physically challenging but it will challenge your faith. You really have to be dead to self and ready at all times to share the reality of God with whoever crosses your path.

I prayed about where to carry the cross. I felt impressed to go to the Orkney Islands just off the north coast of Scotland. I decided to walk from Stromness to Kirkwall which are the two main towns in Orkney, a distance of twelve miles between them – a relatively easy walk. Pastor Andy Frazer met my friend Gordon and me on a cold March morning. A reporter from the Islands' newspaper accompanied Pastor Andy. There was only one other person there on that cold, windy Saturday morning in March as we set off. That person was a woman called Karen, a member of Pastor Andy's congregation. I did a quick interview for the paper and at nine o'clock on the dot I got ready to start my walk.

The streets were deserted; nobody in their right mind would have ventured outside on that cold day. I was excited – both Gordon and I felt privileged to carry the cross – but I was nervous, too. There was a sense of expectancy in the air; anything could happen when carrying the cross. I wondered if people would stop and talk to me. Would it be too heavy for me? Would it hurt my shoulder? I had read somewhere that Arthur Blessitt's collarbone had thickened by a quarter inch from the pressure and pounding of carrying his twelve-foot cross over long distances. He was a lot bigger than my ten-stone, five-foot-six-and-a-half-inch frame. There's only one way to find out, I thought, so I got ready to start walking.

There was a strong wind blowing in from the sea and it was catching the cross, pushing it this way and then that way. I had to hold it firmly to make sure I didn't lose my grip. Andy joked and said I should have put a spoiler on it to keep it on the ground. We prayed together before setting off. I lifted the cross up on my right shoulder and Gordon headed for the car to drive along beside me for a while. I felt like I was heading to the ends of the earth as I started. Orkney has that feel about it, like you're on the edge of the planet. I shouted 'Praise God' at the top of my voice as I picked the cross up on my shoulder.

Immediately there was a flash of lightning, perfectly timed with my first step and, straight after it, a massive roll of thunder which seemed to roll right across the island. The lightning knocked the electricity out on the entire island. Every house went dark and we all stopped in our tracks, even Gordon stopped driving. The hair went up on the backs of our necks. It seemed as if God was stepping down from heaven to join us. Then, immediately after the thunder and lightning, the heavens opened and heavy snow fell. In minutes the road ahead of me was turned into a splendid, spotlessly white carpet of snow. I will never forget that moment for as long as I live. God confirmed my decision to carry the cross. All the criticism I had received from people evaporated in this heaven-sent moment. God and I were a majority once again. I was relieved to be confirmed as not being a flaky Christian with a cross but as a man who had heard from God. I was in his will and very excited.

I continued across the island without further lightning or thunder, just the first one – it was as if God stepped out from heaven and then went in again.

The walk across the island was challenging but not too difficult. I didn't meet many people, as it was extremely cold, so even the hardy islanders didn't venture out. My arms were tired and my shoulders were slightly bruised but nothing too serious. That evening I was speaking at the leisure centre in Kirkwall. I was very expectant that night. I felt that God might turn up at the meeting to bless people. I preached my heart out, but there was absolutely no sense of the presence of God there, none whatsoever. I must admit I was very disappointed; I had really expected God to do something special at the meeting.

It just goes to show, God's ways are not our ways. However, I was about to learn once again that it has absolutely nothing to do with me whether or not God turns up, or even if I can feel or sense his presence. I should just be obedient to his will.

We had a cup of tea with the church leaders in a room at the back of the leisure centre after the meeting. I was about to leave to go and stay at the home of Andy's friend for the night when several of the youth who had attended the meeting came into the room. They asked me to come back into the hall where I had just spoken. The youth wanted to thank me for coming to the island with the cross and they asked me to pray for them. I agreed; of course I was happy to pray for these lovely young Christians.

I walked back into the main hall of the leisure centre where there were about twenty young people already gathered. The youth leader, a young fair-haired local lad, called for quiet. He then began to thank Gordon and me for coming to Orkney and sharing the gospel with them that evening. He then asked me if I would like to pray for them all. 'Of course,' I answered. I thought to myself that I would just pray and then go home. Both Gordon and I were feeling very tired; it had been a long day.

I stayed put on the spot where I was standing. I planned to pray a sincere prayer of blessing over them all. When I prayed I didn't touch any of them or even go very near them, I just opened my mouth to pray when suddenly the glory of God fell in the room. At the same time every one of the youth fell like a collapsing deck of cards to the ground. They didn't just fall; they collapsed, in a heap, all of them. They were all literally vibrating, like they were plugged into an electric current. Never in my life have I seen anything like it – neither before, nor since. They were all filled with the Holy Spirit. Many of their lives were changed forever. They stayed on the ground for over two hours. Strangely I didn't feel the same power in me at all. I went home after about an hour and a half. I stayed that long and just watched them all vibrating under the power of God. I heard the next day that when they finally got back on their feet they all went out on the streets sharing the gospel with people as they came out of the pubs in Kirkwall.

I have met some of them again recently (13 years later) and they still talk with awe of the night that God came to Kirkwall. One of the young men who was touched by God that night lay on the ground for over four hours. His friends had to carry him home. He told me when I was up there two years ago that that day was one of the best days of his entire life. Hallelujah!

Chapter 8
Crosswalk in America

My next walk was to be bigger than anything I had ever done before – America was on my heart. I could not get it out of my mind. I studied it on maps and I showed them to Tricia. We pored over and studied the possible routes together. 'Wow, John, it's such a huge country! Will you manage it?'

'I will manage it, Tricia. God will make a way and give us everything we need to do it.'

Three thousand miles of desert, mountains, cities and wilderness. I painstakingly worked out a route; every detail had to be plotted across the country. I planned to start at the Pacific Ocean near Santa Monica in Los Angeles, walk up through Hollywood, by Beverly Hills, then up over the 8,000-foot San Bernardino Mountains past Big Bear Lake and out into the Mojave Desert, on to the famous Route 66 up through Las Vegas – wow, I couldn't wait to preach there! – on to the Grand Canyon, then south to Oklahoma, across to Memphis, Washington DC, and over the Blue Ridge Mountains of Virginia that I only knew about because of the famous old Laurel and Hardy song.

Continuing on through Philadelphia we planned to finish by the Atlantic Ocean near New York. 'See, Tricia, it's simple,' I said and we laughed together. 'What have I married?' Tricia joked. 'You crazy Irishman.'

I had the faith for it, yet I didn't have the organisational experience for such a walk – as I was to find out.

I trained hard, running out over the hills near Largs in Ayrshire. Mile after mile I trailed up over hills. I even went up to Ben Nevis, the highest mountain in Britain, to run up the 4,000-foot monster of a mountain. I did it in just over an hour and a half. It takes most people over three hours to get to the top! Satisfied that I was fit enough I raised about £3,000 and flew out to LA with Gordon.

Gordon is a big man: he stands at six foot four inches and weighs about nineteen stone. He is a true man of God as well as a great friend who has faithfully served me on many trips. He lives just outside Ayr in Scotland and is married to Helen. They have two children, Stuart and Nicola. I am so grateful for the big man and for his family allowing him to be released to come with me on these mission trips. People call us 'Little and Large'. Gordon has been known to pick me up and hold me over his head when I get cranky with him; he won't put me down until I agree to calm down. I could not have done my walks without him; he was always willing to do whatever needed to be done. Thank you, big man!

I didn't realise it but I still had a lot to learn about faith and walking really long distances. The organisation for a 3,000-mile walk is quite different from walking through the length and breadth of Ireland or Britain. My plan was not great but it was the only plan I had. I didn't have anyone to advise me on how to manage or organise such a long trip on foot. There is faith and there is folly. This time, without realising it, I was stepping out in a mixture of both faith and folly.

I mean, we had no contacts over there, no meetings organised, we did not have enough money to make it across
the USA and, above all, we had no car, caravan or support
vehicle to assist us as we went. The only media contact
we had was with Peter Wooding. At the time Peter was the
news editor with United Christian Broadcasters in Stoke-
on-Trent. He told me that his dad was a journalist in Los
Angeles and that he headed up a Christian communica-
tions organisation called Assist.com. That was all we had
to go on.

I chose to go in September, as that would be the beginning of autumn in America and therefore, I reasoned, it
would not be too hot, nor would it be too cold – at least
that is what I hoped. Gordon and I headed for London
to catch our flights. We met our friends from Dublin at
Heathrow airport: Tommo Curtis and Joe Fitzgerald from
Ireland wanted to join us for the beginning of the walk.

I must tell you that shortly before I left Britain I had
been studying a book called *God's Generals* written by a
guy called Roberts Liardon. He is a Christian historian who
has written extensively about famous men and women of
God, people who were touched and used mightily by the
Holy Spirit.

I was studying the ministry of a woman named Aimee
Semple McPherson. Aimee had been used mightily
by God to start a revival in Los Angeles during the
Great Depression of 1929–39. I was fascinated by this
extraordinary woman, both by her faith and her exploits.
She had, with God's help, built the biggest church in
America – America's first mega church – called Angelus
Temple. Through an amazing set of coincidences (or
God-incidences as I had started calling them) we ended
up staying free of charge in the hostel belonging to and

adjoining her fabulous church. We were due to start the walk the next day, Saturday.

Early Saturday morning, before we left the hostel for the start of the walk, one of the staff from the church came to see me. They told me that the pastor of the famous church had heard about me and requested that I speak in the Sunday morning service. She told me they wanted to pray for me and my team before we left. I felt privileged, particularly because this great church was dedicated to worldwide and interdenominational preaching of the gospel. I knew that in former years Angelus Temple had seen greater days, multitudes had gathered in its pews. The 5,000-seat building had a small congregation of maybe five hundred at that time.

A couple of days before the start of the walk I trudged through the streets and parks surrounding the church. We had no idea that it is actually a very dangerous area to walk through. I walked through the famous Echo Park, speaking to people and sharing the gospel with them. I had no idea that dangerous gangs and criminals hung out in the streets around there. What you don't know won't hurt you, I guess. That's the attitude I have to have, otherwise fear could grip me and I would be frightened to go into certain areas. I knew that I would have to walk in dangerous places, but no matter what colour you are, no matter how dangerous the area is, the cross acts like a passport for me. People do not so much see me but they see the cross.

I walked around Echo Park and the surrounding area, praying that God would do a great work here again. On the eve of the walk I stood outside the famous Angelus Temple. Its great big cross lit up the huge dome on top of the building. I laid hands on the dedication stone which is embedded in one of the large pillars by the steps at the front door of the famous church. I prayed earnestly that

God would do a great work here once again.

Today this building is filled to capacity. It is the church used by Pastor Matthew Barnet and the incredible Dream Centre in Los Angeles.

On the morning of the walk we gathered on the beach beside the famous pier at Santa Monica. There to meet us was Peter Wooding and his father Dan; true to their word they came to interview us at the start of our epic journey. Once the interviews were over we prayed together, asking God to bless our journey and to protect us as we travelled.

I always like to touch the ocean on both ends of a country when we walk through nations, so at that point Gordon and I touched the water in the Pacific Ocean. I then put the eleven-foot cross up on my shoulder and looked along the famous pier; its wooden frame stretched for about two hundred and fifty yards ahead of us before it hit the coast road at Santa Monica. The sun beat down on us as we set off, but there was a cool breeze coming in from the Pacific Ocean which kept us from getting too hot. 'Let God be praised,' I shouted as I took the first steps on our epic trip. I had walked about twenty yards when Dan and Peter Wooding stopped us to put the first of hundreds of signatures on the cross.

Three thousand miles lay before me and I determined that no matter what happened I would finish it. I had thought and prayed for years about this walk and now, at last, it was a reality. I was frightened but excited. I prayed a silent prayer on my first steps that God would save thousands and that he would come to us in his miraculous power to set the addict free and bless millions through our media interviews.

Gordon was a little nervous driving on the American or right side of the road. His concentration was fully on staying safe and subsequently he took a wrong turn right at the very beginning of the trip. I was heading left at the end of the pier. Gordon ended up turning right. Poor Gordon got himself into a right panic and ended up getting lost for several hours on the streets of Santa Monica. This meant I was on my own. I was not too worried, though, as we had cell phones and I knew I could contact him later. I left Gordon to find his way back to me and got on with the job in hand.

The first road I walked on was the coast road at Santa Monica. I had travelled no more than ten yards onto the footpath next to this road when a red sporty Chrysler car pulled up alongside me. A man jumped out and called to me to stop and talk to him. It turned out that he was a journalist from the *Los Angeles Times* and he'd happened to spot me with my cross as he passed the end of the Santa Monica pier. 'May I take some photos of you and do an interview?' he asked. Wow, I thought, if I'd tried to arrange an interview with the *Los Angeles Times* I bet I couldn't have. We did an interview and photo shoot there and then which appeared in the *Los Angeles Times* the next day.

I crossed the road and turned onto Santa Monica Boulevard, up into West Hollywood. The sun was beating down on me; it was already hot and it wasn't even eleven o'clock yet. I was not wearing a hat and I hadn't put any sunscreen on – silly me. I tried to stay on the shaded side of the road so that I wouldn't burn up. Everyone was looking at me with my cross and almost immediately people began to come over to chat. A couple from Hawaii asked me what I was doing so I had a brief chat with them. They shared with me that a close friend of theirs was addicted to drugs and asked me to pray for them. I held their hands and prayed for them and for their friend back home, that God would bless them and set their friend free from drugs. There were tears in their eyes as they thanked me profusely for taking a little time with them.

Many more people stopped me as I continued up the Boulevard towards Los Angeles city. I caught sight of the famous Hollywood sign up on the hills to my left. I must admit I was a little disappointed with Hollywood, it's quite boring compared to the impression we see on telly. I discerned three distinct atmospheres as we travelled through the famous streets. The first was an atmosphere that oozed promiscuity. I learned that there are over two thousand homeless gay youth that sleep on the streets in this area. Forty-one percent of the population in West Hollywood is gay and the majority of the local town council are gay too. I spoke to many people in this gay community as they sat in the shade of kerbside bars and coffee houses. Many of them had come from all over the world to Hollywood to make it as film stars or to get their break in the film industry. Some of them were very open to the gospel. A couple of English gay guys spoke to me about their family back home and how they missed them. I met one guy who was with an obviously rich older gay man. The older man was very disrespectful to him while we chatted and I could see that the younger guy longed to come home and be away from here and be with his family again in England. I offered to pray for them but the older guy wouldn't have it. 'There is no God,' he said. 'We are gods of our own lives.' I could see the younger guy wanted me to pray. I left, but prayed for them on the way up the road.

I was reminded of Psalms 14:1: 'The fool says in his heart, "There is no God."' I wondered how many people had come to Hollywood to try and make it in the film industry and had ended up on the boulevard of broken dreams.

Rehabilitation and Homosexuality

Please allow me to digress for a moment to share important experiences I had many years ago.

I was reminded of a time when I was homeless back in the seventies and eighties in London. I used to write letters home to my parents and tell them I was doing well, that I had a nice girlfriend, a good flat and a steady job. I had none of these things – in reality I was living on the streets. I did not want my parents to worry about me and, of course, I wanted them to have some pride in me. I could not tell them the truth about how things really were. I am sure many of the homeless and unemployed even in Hollywood write similar letters or emails to worried parents back home.

I know that when you live a long way from home, that if you hit hard times you become vulnerable. Some people may try to take advantage of you when you are in this position. I remember on several occasions meeting some predatory-type people on the streets of London who would try their utmost to take advantage of you. Older gay guys would try to seduce you, buying you drinks and making promises that they would help you to get home or get a job – they would try anything to win your confidence. Their ultimate aim is to try to have sex with you and they go to no ends to try and make that happen. I shared in my book *Walking Free* how at one time I was raped while I was co-matose on both drugs and drink. They try to convince you that you too are gay. I thank God that even in the midst of my addiction, vulnerability and pain that I did not allow these people to influence me or to take me into this life-style. I ran from them every time I met them, except for that one time when I was raped.

This is a world that not many people know about; the politically correct lobbyists of today know nothing of this

gutter life. These predators prayed on many of the homeless and lonely people I knew on the streets; these homeless guys were straight when I knew them. These horrible
people would ply the homeless with drink or drugs and
they would offer them a home or, more likely, a bed for
the night. The tired and hungry homeless would take the
bait, but when they were alone with them they would try
to convince them that they were gay, too. They would say,
'Everyone has a gay side, and it's alright to experiment
with it.' I hated it when I came across these perverted men.
We were all vulnerable guys, looking for acceptance from
society. These guys hung around the squats we frequented
or the streets we lived on. We were homeless, hungry and
hurting, often shy homeless guys. We were not gay but, in
my experience, these men tried to manipulate the thoughts
of my friends and me to turn us into fodder for their selfish
sexual desires. I did not succumb to their persuasions but
I witnessed many other young guys and girls fall for it.

Some of these guys ended up as rent boys on the streets
of London. I must say I get frustrated and worry when I feel
the pressure of being politically incorrect when addressing
this issue. Gay people in my experience are usually very
nice, decent people. I am amazed, though, how many of
them have problems with their past, have histories of sexual, physical or emotional abuse, bad relationships with
their fathers, or else have no father figure whatsoever in
their lives. Some of them, too, may have come across gay
guys who try to persuade them that it's OK to experiment
with sex and sexuality. Before they know it they try it and
become convinced by others that they, too, are gay. Now
our government has been convinced by lobbyists to bring
teaching in to our schools, telling our children it's OK to
sleep with the same sex. How far will this go?

I also remember a time when I attended a rehabilitation

centre in Uxbridge just outside London. It was a male rehab called Suffolk House, run under the Phoenix House rehabilitation organisation model. Every night we recited their philosophy. We would gather in the living room, about fifteen men, and put our arms around each other (in a manly way) and recite this philosophy:

We are here because there is no refuge finally from ourselves. Until we confront ourselves, in the eyes and hearts of others we shall be running. Here at last, we can appear clearly unto ourselves, not as the giant of our dreams, nor as the dwarf of our fears, but as humans. Part of a whole, with a share in its purpose. Here together we can each take root and grow, not alone as in death, but alive to ourselves and to each other.

This philosophy sounds great but in reality the rehabilitation centre was a complete nightmare. They experimented with all kinds of therapies, confrontation groups, marathon relaxation classes, levitation, contacting the dead and allowing them to speak to us through the leader of the rehab. Then they decided to experiment with sexuality. It seemed there was no escape from homosexuality during these times, whether it was out on the streets being pursued by gay predators or whether it was in rehab during the late seventies and early eighties. The world was changing and it was us in the underworld who were seeing and feeling the sexual and new age change in society's trends.

One day the trustees of the rehab – they were all upper-middle-class women, women who didn't have a clue about how we lived or thought – told us that from that day they would be bringing women into the centre; that from then on it would be a mixed rehab home. That was difficult enough to deal with, but then a few weeks later they told us that we would all be allowed, and even encouraged, to experiment with our sexuality. They told us that the men would be allowed to wear make-up and dress in women's clothes while we were in the rehab house, and the women would be allowed to dress in men's clothes, cut their hair and behave like men.

Oh my word! The next few months were like a micro-cosm of what the world has become since the seventies. I could see how crazy it was and therefore I never took part in any of the shenanigans that went on in the house. I considered leaving the centre before they embarked on these new experimental types of rehabilitation methods. I decided to stay for a while and see if I could navigate the changes within the rehab. The only other option I had open to me was to return to the streets of London to a life of homelessness and addiction.

I still feel angry when I remember the manipulation and deception that went on in these types of rehabs. Who the hell did these people think we were? Amazingly now I see our governments doing the same things in society, and society, just like in the rehab, is accepting it.

At the beginning of this season, when the girls arrived, we all got on really well. Now some of them had been prostitutes or call girls, pretty girls, so you can imagine the goings on down in the garden shed; guys with girls making out behind the washing machine at the back of the shed. The difficulties, confrontations and bad atmospheres this brought into the rehab made it very difficult to keep focused on getting our lives together.

Then the cross-dressing started. For crying out loud, you had men dressed as women and women dressed as men. They still went down the garden shed making out but now some of them were making out homosexually; it was very disconcerting and very worrying. I was very upset by it all – what chance did we have of staying drug free when all this confusion, unnecessary in my eyes, was going on? One guy even left at this time and committed suicide. We were not allowed to speak against the goings on in the rehab; it was considered to be insensitive or cruel to make fun of or complain about the developments within our rehab during this time. The only time we could complain was within the confines of the confrontation group or in a one-to-one meeting with the head staff. However, the staff were promoting this new so-called enlightened breakthrough in rehab and we did not get much of a hearing or support when we complained.

I will never forget the morning when Tony (a tall, strong, red-haired guy from Yeovil in Somerset) appeared at the top of the stairs. I was at the bottom, cleaning and doing my morning duties. Tony shouted down the stairs at me, saying, 'John Edwards, don't you say a word to me this morning about how I'm dressed. I'm experimenting with my sexuality.' I lifted my head up to look at Tony. He was at the top of the stairs. You should have seen him: he was dressed in a long, light blue and white floral patterned dress which came down to just below his knees. One of the fat upper-middle-class trustees must have left it for us. Anyway ... Tony had on a pair of high-heels which must have been three-inches high, making him totter precariously at the top of the stairs, standing at about six-foot-six. He had red rouge type make-up on his cheeks, blue eyeliner and black mascara plus, the final touch, lovely orange lipstick. He began to waltz, or mince, down the stairs. I am afraid I could not hold the laughter in. I literally collapsed on the floor laughing – oh, I laughed till it hurt. He was the funniest sight I had seen in months.

Tony's face flushed with rage. He began to shout at me. The amazing thing was that his body language was effeminate; he had all the hand gestures and was swinging his hips like he was a woman. This made me worse. I realised I was being insensitive; homophobia or political correctness were unknown terms back then but I could feel the angry stares from a couple of the others on the programme. I looked into the office where some of the other rehab students were, only to see the motley crew of mixed genders glaring at me. Men dressed like women with make-up on and women dressed like men with short hair and no make-up. It was like a scene from that crazy pub in the *Star Wars* movie.

Tony went into the staff office to hide from me and the stares of the rest of the gang. That afternoon we had a group meeting; it was our usual confrontation group. Well, I'm not exaggerating when I say that during this group the claws came out. I got slammed by them all for being so insensitive to Tony. They wanted, even demanded to know why I wouldn't experiment with my sexuality. They couldn't seem to accept that although I was an addict and an alcoholic I was secure in my sexuality. That evening the whole conversation in the living room turned to sexual fantasies, the motley crew of gender mixed cross-dressers talked excitedly about their sexual fantasies. I won't go into any detail about those conversations here but to say that they were off the charts is not an exaggeration. That evening I decided to leave the rehab. I could not stay there another day; it was worse than a circus.

I witnessed how Tony and all the others who experimented with their sexuality immediately took on a persona that was not them. Cross-dressing was like wearing a mask: the body language took on a gay stance; they minced around the rehab in a confidence that was not rooted in who they really were. When I see a picture of a crying clown or of a clown on television with a sad look on his face, I am always reminded of Suffolk House rehab. I believe that we in rehabs were used as guinea pigs in the changing society and sexual revolution of the seventies and eighties. I have heard of a number of these people who died after they left rehab. I left that rehab shortly after the above episode.

I returned to the West End of London and slept on the streets again; it was only a couple of days before I went back on drugs. However, homelessness and drug abuse were more normal to me than the mixed-up gender madness of rehab at Suffolk House.

I vowed never to go to rehab again but, thank God, I changed that vow and found Teen Challenge about twelve years later. Because of God's work in me at Teen Challenge I am alive, married, confident, happy and fulfilled in who I am. This is because I took the time to look into the truth of the Bible and finally was able to experience freedom. Hallelujah! Rehabilitation doesn't work. Regeneration does...

Back to My American Walk

Back to my walk in America again ... I passed a plaque on a wall in West Hollywood that commemorated the Stonewall riots of 1969. I stopped here for a while, laid the cross against the plaque and prayed for the gay community: that the lonely, hurting and suicidal amongst them would find help and freedom.

When I finished praying I headed west towards the city. I was getting nearer to Los Angeles. The skyscrapers stood proud in the midst of this sad smoggy city. There are 90,000 homeless in this city, yet when we see Los Angeles on TV we associate it with success, movies, money, fame and freedom. How wrong we are. I knew that I was carrying the answer to the world's problems on my shoulders. That message is the cross and the answer the cross brings to a lost and dying world. I have seen the witchcraft, poverty and darkness of India, experienced the power of Satan during my lifetime, but none of it equals the darkness we have in our western cities.

Many gathered round me and the cross to find out what I was doing. I was able to share with literally hundreds of people, many of whom asked me to pray for them and then signed their names on the cross. I would not let anyone put their names on the cross unless they took the gospel message seriously and allowed me to pray with them.

I was wearing denim, knee-length shorts and by this time the sun had shifted and it was beginning to burn. The shorts were cutting into the back of my sweaty, sunburned legs. I had much to learn about walking in America. I had stupidly forgotten to take money – Gordon had the money and he was still lost in LA – so I couldn't even buy myself a bottle of water. I had been relying on Gordon meeting me along the route for water breaks, but he was still lost somewhere in Santa Monica.

Met By an Angel?

On one street intersection, as I was waiting to cross the road, a group of about ten people gathered around me. While I was talking and praying with them I noticed this guy come up to the kerb on a racing bike. He was powerfully built, had platinum-blond, shoulder-length hair, and I noticed that he looked like he didn't shave, or rather didn't need to shave. His face was smooth, not smooth like a baby's but with a wax-like quality about it. I estimated he was close to thirty years of age. He stared at me for ages, his blue eyes were filled with peace. I wondered who he was. Why was he looking at me like that? It was a little unnerving.

I finished praying with the people who had gathered

round me. The guy staring at me then got off his bike and came over to me. 'Can I talk to you, sir?' he asked in a polite soft voice. 'Yes, of course,' I replied. He immediately began to relate to me this amazing story about a supernatural place in God that can be experienced if we will pay the price of dying to self. His conversation was so deep I could not understand or follow some of it. I asked him to come round the corner into the shade to talk. The sun had moved completely to my side of the street and there was no escaping its rays; my legs were burning and getting sore.

When we got round the corner into the shade he took up his amazing conversation where he had left off. There was something different about this guy but I couldn't quite put my finger on it. I really enjoyed speaking with him, even though his conversation was hard to understand. Suddenly he finished speaking and said that he had to go. I asked if I could pray with him before he departed. 'Of course,' he replied. I put my right hand on his left shoulder. When I did so he placed his head on my left shoulder and then he began to sob. He just sobbed and sobbed for the whole time I prayed for him and even when I finished he kept his head there. I was a bit embarrassed and not sure what to do. It must have looked really strange, even by Hollywood standards: a little Irish guy in silly shorts, sunburned and white skinny legs, an eleven-foot cross leaning against my side, and with a burly blond guy crying on my shoulder. Then he lifted his head, thanked me and got back on his bike. 'Bye, John, I'll see you later,' he said as he cycled off. I wondered how he would see me later when he didn't even know what direction I was headed in. I hadn't shared with him the route I was taking through the city.

I continued walking. There was still no sign of Gordon so I had to go into shops and cafés to ask them for water to drink to keep myself hydrated. The sun was hot and there was little shade. I continued up through Hollywood, down through Beverly Hills, sharing the gospel with some very wealthy-looking people. I continued down by a lovely round raised pond that I sat at and dangled my feet in for a while to cool down. A man came out from behind a tree near the pond. He was a tramp; all his belongings were in a big brown and dirty canvas sack he dragged behind him. He came to the pond and began washing his face in the clear water. I started a conversation with him and prayed for him before I carried on walking. I thought it ironic that in Beverly Hills, one of the wealthiest parts of the world, the first person I should pray with was a poor homeless man. I moved on again, talking to many as I went. I'm not very well up on film stars but some of the people I spoke to looked vaguely familiar. I then carried on through to Sunset Boulevard.

'Gordon, where are you?' I prayed. I went through a stretch of road where there were no shops or cafés that I could get water in. I needed a drink: my mouth was dry and my body was dehydrating. I hadn't planned for that. I was now overheating, too. The cross is heavy and when I have carried it for several miles it begins to hurt my shoulders.

I then met two genuine Navajo Indians. They stopped me and I spent fifteen minutes with them, leading them both to the Lord. Wow! Real Indians – I'd never seen any before except on the cowboy films.

I came to another street intersection. The street was wide and, as I waited to cross the road, a man came up to me for a chat. He told me that he was a Jew. I chatted with him for about fifteen minutes and as I finished the conversation with him I prayed a silent prayer: 'Lord, please, I need a long cold drink.' Immediately after I prayed this prayer, out of nowhere it seemed, my burly blond-haired friend on the bike appeared with a can of freezing cold tomato juice in his hand. Before I could say anything he had put it in my hand. I was stunned by this immediate answer to prayer. He hadn't stopped though. I looked behind me to see where he had gone to. He was nowhere to be seen. He couldn't have just vanished, or gone out of my sight so quickly. I was flabbergasted! Opening the cold can of tomato juice I remembered that earlier I had asked him if he would like to write his name on my cross, just like many others had done. 'No, thank you. Maybe later, John,' he had said.

'What is your name?' I'd asked him.

'Michael Gabriel,' he had replied. Suddenly it struck me: his hair, build, smooth skin on his face, those eyes. Michael Gabriel, I pondered ... had I just been given a cold drink of tomato juice by an angel? Possibly.

Just then Gordon drove up in the car. 'Boy, am I glad to see you?' I said. Poor old Gordon had spent the first day of our trip lost in Los Angeles. We finished walking for the day and went back to our hostel at Angelus Temple. What a day it had been – I was so excited. Tommo, Joe, Gordon and I spent the evening chatting enthusiastically about the day's events. Before retiring for the night, Tommo went to Wal-Mart and bought me some sun cream, a hat to protect me from the sun, a tent for later on in the desert, and a water bottle that I could carry with me. I also got out some lightweight long trousers to protect my legs from the sun. I took the cross apart and we retired for the evening. We all slept well and woke early the next morning.

It was Sunday morning and I was speaking in Angelus Temple. I was excited at the prospect of speaking in such a large, famous and historic building. God had orchestrated this for me; I felt honoured and privileged, not just because

I was speaking in such a famous church building but more so because I had a terrific sense that God was with me and he had planned it all. I decided to bring the cross into the service with me.

The pastor welcomed us all into the church and, after the powerful worship, he invited me up to speak from the famous platform. I shared my testimony and told the congregation of our plans to walk across America with the cross. Looking out at the scattered five-hundred-plus congregation I hoped and prayed that this church would see better days and be filled to capacity again in the near future. I held my cross up high for some of my message. As I spoke the sense of God with me was awesome.

The Word Gets Out

Over the next couple of days I walked up through Riverside and on up towards the San Bernardino Mountains. I managed to walk up the 8,000-foot mountains without too much difficulty; the air was a bit thin near the top but I coped well. I stood on top of the mountain with my cross held high, looking down on the City of Angels, a heavy grey and yellow smog covered the fabulous city. I stopped for half an hour and prayed for God's blessing to fall on the city and for the lost and addicted to find hope in God.

The last few days had been incredible. I had never in my life seen so many miracles happen! The media had hold of the story and my mobile phone was ringing all the time now. Journalists from radio stations, magazines and newspapers got in touch, not only from America but from New Zealand, Australia and Europe, too. The word was getting out. People had been stopping in their cars, getting out and kneeling on the pavement, crying in repentance and asking Christ to come into their hearts. Some who saw me on TV or heard me on radio came looking for me, and radio stations began to monitor my walk day by day. People were phoning in asking how the little Irish man with the cross was getting on. People got saved, delivered and filled with the Holy Spirit daily.

Into the Desert

I will never forget the sense of awe that took hold of me as I began to descend the San Bernardino Mountains. I walked around one particular bend and there before me was a panoramic view of the Mojave Desert, 8,000 feet below and stretching as far as the eye could see, Joshua trees dotted everywhere. All I could see was mile after mile of sand. I gasped, taking in the magnitude of my journey. Doubt and fear gripped me. Would I be able to make it? Would Gordon and I get across the desert? 'Come on, John!' I told myself. 'Speak faith to yourself.' I had only a hire car, a small amount of money, and a lot of faith. That should be enough.

I started down, into the oven-hot desert and, lifting the cross on my back, I fixed my face like flint and off I went. I had my bottle of water strapped to my side and a good floppy hat to protect my balding head from the desert sun. I prayed in tongues for the next few miles, praying for God to strengthen me as I went.

Chapter 9
Fighting Dogs and
Desert Addicts

I had one terrifying experience when I had walked only a few miles into the desert. The narrow tarmac road was completely covered in sand. Trailers, occupied by old hippie types, were dotted here and there. I saw a couple of dogs running loose in the distance. There were no fences on these houses and trailers, and some of the dogs were quite large. Fear gripped me as I saw one of them spot me. I picked up a dead tree branch that lay in the sand nearby. It was sun bleached, about two-feet long and maybe two-inches in diameter. I thought if one of the dogs came for me I could ram the stick in its mouth or hit it on the head until Gordon came for me. He was just a mile ahead of me making lunch on the side of the desert road. Tommo and Joe had returned to Ireland just before we began climbing the San Bernardino Mountains.

Just then the dog began to run at full pelt towards me. 'Oh Jesus,' I cried, 'please protect me.' I was sure that this dog would try to rip me to shreds and was even more horrified when he came closer. It was a Pit Bull Terrier; they are one of the most vicious fighting dogs you can find. I put the cross on the ground in front of me, between me and the dog, and held the stick up in my right hand with my left arm out in front of me. My plan was to let the dog grab my left arm, then to hit him as hard as I could on the head with the stick, hopefully knocking him out.

I was surprised at how calm I was when all that stood between me and this running, barking, fighting dog was the cross, a stick and faith. On and on the dog ran, then just as he got near to me, about three feet away and just on the other side of the cross, the big animal stopped, looked a bit puzzled at me, then began to wag his tail and lick me all over. Phew, I gasped a sigh of relief. 'Oh thank you so much, Jesus.' I hoisted the cross on my shoulder again and continued walking. The dog stayed with me until I reached the first little town in the Mojave Desert, a town called Lucerne Valley.

There was nobody around. I looked up and down the main street: it was empty, not a person in sight. Then I spotted some cars at the back of a dusty old Four Square church just a little further up the road. The back door of the church was open and I could see some people getting out of an old beat-up Chevy and going into the building.

I walked on over towards the church and, as I got closer, I noticed a sign on the open door. I couldn't believe my eyes. It read 'Narcotics Anonymous'. Ha! An NA meeting. I parked my cross outside and stepped into the room. The light was dim inside and there was a smell of stale sweat mixed with tobacco smoke. I estimated that there were about twenty people sitting in the room.

As I entered they all turned their heads to look at me – big, burly, tattooed, hairy Americans, addicts and ex-addicts, all looking at me. Their faces were a picture! I wish I'd had my camera with me. A photo of their faces would have been one to keep and show the grandkids. I must have been a sight to behold: a little Irish guy in my fancy Nike trainers, white socks, and lightweight slacks to keep the sun off my legs. On my head I wore a large floppy grey hat and my face was sunburned. I noticed some of them looking behind me at my eleven-foot wooden cross which I had parked outside the door of the meeting room. This only caused more looks of bewilderment.

I sat down without saying a word. Silence reigned momentarily. One girl gave me a cup of water. I must have looked like I needed it. I decided I had better break the silence. 'Hello,' I said. 'My name is John and I'm an ex-addict from Dublin in Ireland. I just happened to be passing. I'm walking across America carrying that cross outside and bringing the good news to addicts, that Jesus loves them and wants to set them free.'

I stopped speaking then, the air was pregnant with questions. Then one of them, a big guy at the far end of the room, shouted a great big, 'Hallelujah!' Someone else said 'Praise God.' Woo hoo, some of them were Christians. I had a great time with these people. They invited Gordon and me into their houses and trailers and they looked after us. They fed us and, in return, we taught them from the Bible, helping them to understand the Scriptures. Every day Gordon drove ahead of me and I walked across the desert, out towards Arizona. Every evening for about five days we returned to our friends at Lucerne Valley. Then on the sixth day we left them.

Many of the former addicts came to bid us farewell. One of them came over to me and said, 'Will you please keep in touch with us, John? You understand us, you speak our language, we understand the Bible when you speak to us. We don't have anyone to support us or teach us the way you can.' I would have loved to stay longer with them but I just had to move on.

When I stayed with them or when I visited their homes and trailers I noticed that they all had computers and the Internet in their homes. While thinking and praying about them after I left, I wondered if there was any way I could help them. Then I got an amazing idea: imagine if I was able to set up a virtual reality rehabilitation programme that could help people like them. There must be millions of addicts around the world needing spiritual help. I believe the Internet holds great potential as part of the answer for people like that. I have now written great lessons and structures that would work on the Internet. All I need is some people who have the technology, skills and finance to help get it up and going.

It turned out that I had walked into the area where methamphetamine is illegally made. I was told that 70% of the people in the area were involved in the illegal manufacture of it. What a miracle it was that I should walk into their midst with my cross. I will never forget these people. They made a collection for us before we left them, giving us $160 for our cross-walk.

Chapter 10
Wits' End

Gordon and I had been sleeping in the tent out in the desert. We knew that snakes and scorpions were about, but we were committed to the journey. Man, the difficulties we encountered over those few days in Lucerne Valley were tremendous. The road began to vanish under sand with hills so steep that eventually the little car couldn't cope. The car wheels were spinning on the sand, Gordon and I had to sweep the sand off the potholed tarmac and then turn the car around and reverse it up the hill, keeping the weight of the engine under the front-drive wheels. That was the only way up and then at the top of the hill he had to turn the car round again to drive down the far side. We kept doing this until we got way out in the desert. Eventually the roads got so bad that we just could not continue, yet I was absolutely determined to go on.

That night we pitched the tent in the desert then drove the car off the road onto the sand. I put the full headlights on, took my Bible out and read aloud the story of Abraham, how God had promised him a son. God had told Abraham to count the stars. I looked up at the desert sky, it was magnificent; thousands of stars sparkled in the dark and clear sky. God had told Abraham to count the stars, and then he told him to look at the grains of sand. As many as there are 'so shall your offspring be'. I counted until I could count no more. 'God,' I shouted into the desert night. 'These are the amount of people I believe you want me to reach.' I pleaded in faith for God to make a way for us to keep going.

I will never forget that night. Never before had I stepped out so far in faith. I was learning many lessons. I should have planned better, should have had a four-wheel drive vehicle, not a little white front-wheel drive car. The voices of my critics screamed loud in my mind. I comforted myself with the thought that at least I had tried. I had already reached thousands. 'Lord, I praise you in all I do,' I shouted into the desert night. 'Please make a way where there seems to be no way. I will go to the ends of the earth if you want me to. Yes, Lord, I will go. I will go, even if it doesn't make sense to me or my friends. I will obey your voice, for I know that even you learned obedience through what you suffered.'

I knew that Jesus didn't follow logic; he followed his father's voice, often going to solitary places and into the desert. As I read my Bible in my tent that night, a sand storm had blown up and was raging outside. Poor Gordon was struggling. I prayed for him. I searched the Scriptures and saw in Hebrews 11 that Abraham, Isaac and Jacob had wandered in deserts, sleeping in tents. We were in good company. I had a sense of identification with these patriarchs of the faith. Boy I had stepped out far this time, so far out in faith. I didn't sleep well that night, tossing and turning, a war between faith and fear battled for supremacy in my mind.

The desert storm blew all that night, too. Sand was getting in through every tiny hole in our tent; even though we had closed the tent up as tight as we possibly could, still the sand managed to get in. It was in our hair, our mouths, in all our clothes, everywhere – even the car had a film of dusty sand covering the inside. That night I touched something in God that I cannot explain. I had stepped out, believed God against all the odds and I still had hope. I still believed I'd finish the walk but I now knew that I would have to reorganise myself.

Next morning we looked at our maps again. We drove back and round onto Route 66 and I walked on it for a long way. The sun was so hot I was drinking gallons of water, pouring lots over my head to try and keep cool. I had to do this every half mile or so. The going was tough; I still had nearly 2,500 miles to go. I got so exhausted, so tired that eventually I knew I could go no further.

I prayed like I have never prayed before, looking for God to make a way. I felt in my heart that I had to go home soon, but before I did I should carry the cross in Las Vegas and up by the Grand Canyon. How I didn't get heat stroke, I don't know. We weren't far from Death Valley, one of the hottest parts on the entire earth. God was looking after us, that much I knew. Our money was running out too. We had been eating and cooking out in the desert and the sand even got into our food.

Finally I had to give in, but not before going to sin city – Las Vegas. I took great pleasure carrying my eleven-foot cross up the famous strip in Vegas, past all the famous casinos: Caesar's Palace, Bellagio's, Stardust and the Golden Nugget. I was almost arrested in the middle of Vegas for speaking outside a casino because the casino security said I was making their customers uncomfortable and that if I didn't move on they would call the police. One of the security guards was a Christian and he asked me to pray with him. Before I left, he wrote his name on the cross. I met many people that wanted prayer in sin city, people from all over the world. I even met some Irish girls who were over for a wild weekend and they thought that they wouldn't meet anyone they knew in Vegas, although it turned out that they lived just a hundred yards from my mum's house in Dublin. I think that kind of spoiled things a bit for them. I certainly gave them something to think about.

We stayed in Vegas for two days. What a fantastic place it is; I found it to be absolutely inspirational. This is a city that logic and reason tell us should not be there. It's in the middle of the Nevada desert where there are no natural resources to support a city of its size. I wondered what kind of people had planned and pioneered it. What kind of people were they? What motivated them to begin the building of such a place in the desert? Where did they expect to get their business from and where would they get water and light from? And, last but not least, how would people get there in the first place? In the early days there would have been no roads into or out of the area. These pioneering people must have stood there one day and let their imagination just go out as far as they could, and then they built it believing that people would come. Las Vegas was built to fulfil the lust, greed and the need within man for escape and entertainment. I couldn't help thinking that if ungodly people can build a city like this, how much more could we as Christians do if we would have the vision and ability to act in faith and unity?

We finished our outreach to Las Vegas then we drove up by the Hoover Dam, which is where Vegas gets its water. Gordon and I did the tourist thing and took a trip around the incredible famous dam. I am amazed at man, how he can visualise such gigantic projects and persevere with them until they are completed. Of course many of the men who built the dam were customers in the early gambling joints of Las Vegas. Many of the men lost their lives during the building of this manmade wonder of the world.

Leaving here we headed up towards Flagstaff, doing some more newspaper and radio interviews on the way. There were still potentially millions of people hearing about our epic journey across America. We had planned to go to the Grand Canyon before returning to Los Angeles and home. I knew I needed to come home; I had learned a huge lesson of faith. It was humbling to realise that I could not finish the trip with the level of organisation to date. Gordon and I were missing our wives and families. I kept in touch with Tricia every chance I got but she had been worried, of course, and was delighted I was planning on coming home soon. This walk had been a life-changing challenge. I had stepped out in faith, but found myself lacking in organisation and planning skills. I would return at a later date to finish the walk ... that much I knew.

Miracle at Grand Canyon

Growing deep within my soul was an urgency to get to the Grand Canyon. Yes, of course we were excited at the prospect of seeing it for the first time, but something deeper was driving me. I felt as if God wanted me to get there quickly, like there was a specific purpose for us there. We had planned to sleep in our tent, pitching it as near to the edge of the Grand Canyon as possible. Gordon and I wanted to watch the sun rise over it the next morning. That had been a dream of mine and it was about to happen.

We drove through the gates of the national park and headed straight for the village where we planned to pitch our tent. On our arrival we parked our car and, being un-able to restrain ourselves, we immediately ran over to the edge of the canyon. We were like excited children on Christmas morning running down to see what Santa had brought them. We knew a treat awaited us. Breath-taking is an understatement. We stood with eyes wide and mouths open as we tried to drink in the splendour of this magnificent work of God's creation. How wonderful it is to have a relationship with the one who actually made this. Praises to God poured from our lips as we tried to utter appreciation to God for loving us so much and for giving us such a treat. We stood there for nearly an hour taking in the view.

Thirst dictated a need for a cold drink so we sauntered over to a nearby hotel. We were in a town called Grand Canyon Village and situated on the edge of the canyon was a beautiful five-star hotel called the El Tovar Hotel. I sensed the holy presence of God come upon me as I got nearer the hotel building. 'What is it, God?' I asked under my breath as I felt that still, small voice speak to my heart: 'John, there is someone here I want you to meet and help. I want you to stay here tonight and it will be paid for.'

I could not believe what I was hearing: God wanted me to stay here. How could we pay for it? We only had a few hundred dollars left. The El Tovar was a five star hotel. We could not afford it. But, I also knew that God had spoken to me. I had learned from experience to know and recognise his voice.

Gordon and I walked into the hotel. There was a picture of President Clinton on the wall as we went in. He had stayed there a couple of months before. This hotel was a national landmark – fashioned after a European hunting lodge, it was filled with antiques, Indian murals and buffalo heads hung on the walls. 'This place will cost a fortune to stay in. How is God going to organise this?' I wondered. I knew that God had spoken though and I was getting excited. This is why I had felt the urgency to get here. 'OK, God,' I whispered, 'show me what to do.'

I told Gordon what I believed God had said. Good, faithful friend that Gordon is, he never questioned me on this issue. He just laughed a bit and said, 'John Edwards, if God has spoken and wants us to stay here I'm not complaining, it's much better than sleeping in our tent. But, John,' Gordon said, 'we have hardly any money.'

'I know, Gordon,' I replied. 'Let's see how much it is, OK?'

With that I walked over to the reception desk where there were two girls working. One was in her mid-twenties, she was dark haired and quite pretty; the other was in her late forties, she too was attractive, fair haired yet a little tense looking, I thought, like she had something on her mind. She was busy on the phone. The younger girl asked me how she could help and I asked her if there were any rooms available for the night. 'I'm afraid not, sir,' she replied, 'but we do have two suites left.' I gulped as my faith was challenged. I looked at Gordon; he was smiling at me, knowing I was challenged. Now the question came as it always does in moments like these: would I see this through or would I back out?

The Holy Spirit is a gentleman: he doesn't force us to obey his voice; he looks for willing and available people. I looked up at the balcony over my head, trying to buy time to gather my thoughts and faith. A huge buffalo head hung on the wall under the balcony; the buffalo's eyes seemed to be looking straight down at me. Strange things go through my mind at times like this. 'What are you looking at?' I said to myself – it was like he was daring me, goading me.

'Sir, will you be wanting a suite of rooms?' I quickly snapped out of my daydreaming and glanced over at Gordon, hoping he would take the responsibility of the situation away from me. He just smiled that great big smile of his again. The beggar, I thought, he's enjoying this. 'Sir,' the receptionist said again, 'will you be wanting a suite?'

I gave her my attention, 'Erm,' I stuttered, 'how much is a suite of rooms?' She was so gracious, I'm sure we didn't look like we could afford a suite of rooms. 'They're $190 dollars for the night,' she answered. I hesitated, buying time, and asked her if that included breakfast? 'No, sir,' the receptionist answered, 'that price does not include breakfast.'

Gordon couldn't hold it in, he laughed and had to turn away to save my face. I had to make a decision. The older receptionist had now finished making her call. She came over to us and asked if there was a problem. 'Er, no ma'am, there's no problem. I was just booking a suite of rooms for the night.' There, I had done it. I'm now either in big trouble or else I'm about to see God work a miracle, I thought.

I handed the girl my Bank of America card and she began to take care of the transaction. I thought to myself that now I had committed to booking the suite I may as well tell the girls who I was and why I was staying at the hotel.

'May I share something with you?' I asked the girls. 'Of course,' they replied. I'm sure they were curious about what this sunburned little Irish guy and his big pal were doing staying in a hotel they obviously couldn't afford. We must have looked like a comedy act. Gordon is six-foot-four-inches tall, weighs about nineteen stone and I am five-foot-six and weigh about 10 stone. 'Little and Large' some people call us.

I continued telling the receptionists the reason we were here. 'I'm staying here tonight because I believe God wants me to meet someone.' The two girls looked up at me, a little startled by my statement. I continued, 'My name is John, I'm an ex-drug addict and I'm carrying an eleven-foot-long wooden cross right across America, bringing a message of hope and salvation to American people, but especially for the addict and those looking for freedom.'

I had no sooner got the words out of my mouth when the older receptionist's mouth opened. 'You are doing what?' she said. She looked like someone had punched her in the stomach. She then fell back into the chair that, thankfully, was just behind her. She burst into tears, sobbing almost uncontrollably; I knew that this must be the girl God wanted me to meet. Ha! God is amazing; he looks for us to be willing to possibly look like a fool before he shows his hand.

The young receptionist quickly ran to comfort her colleague. I had succeeded in upsetting the entire reception staff in the El Tovar Hotel and I didn't even have the keys to our suite yet. The girl who was crying managed to pull herself together after a few moments. She then stood up and straightened her uniform, walked over to where I was standing and said, 'Sir, may I talk to you for a moment.'

'Of course,' I replied. She came out from behind the reception desk and brought me to a quiet corner to speak to me.

'My name is Lorrie,' she explained. I shook her hand, 'Nice to meet you, Lorrie. My name is John. What's going on?' I asked.

'John,' she continued, 'I have been working here for only three weeks. Just before I started working here I was released from prison for drug dealing and armed robbery. I am an addict, but have managed to stay clean since coming out of prison. I am trying to start a new life here in El Tovar.' She paused to catch her breath and compose herself, then she continued, 'I became a born-again Christian just before I came out of prison.' She started crying again as she explained how she had nearly fallen back on drugs just the day before, less than twenty-four hours ago. I waited for her to pull herself together. 'John, I got on my knees last night in my room and prayed. I asked God to please send me someone to help me because I know that if I don't get help I will go back on drugs again, and if I do I'll die. I just do not have another recovery in me.'

She was sobbing now. I took hold of her arm and led her just round the corner, behind a dividing wall in the hotel lobby, away from the prying eyes of people who had begun to sense all was not well with Lorrie. Just then the amazing sense of the presence of God came upon us. God turned up; he touched Lorrie right there in the middle of the El Tovar Hotel at the Grand Canyon. God had heard Lorrie as she prayed in her room and now he had answered her prayer.

I am sure this is why I had that sense of urgency to get to the Grand Canyon. Oh, how important it is to pay attention to these promptings of the Holy Spirit; people's lives may depend on it.

I prayed with her there and then and God immediately set her free. The conscious presence of Christ the Deliverer came upon her as I prayed. If ever you have been caught in a situation like this, when someone is broken and sincerely ready for God to touch their lives, you will sense that amazing presence of Christ the Deliverer. It is totally God; we are so privileged to be participants with him in situations like this. The glory is only his. Gordon and I left Lorrie then but arranged to meet her later for a chat and a coffee.

Big Gordon and I went out to our car to get our bags and chatted excitedly about Lorrie and what God had just done as we carried them up to our suite. Our suite turned out to be the best one in the entire hotel: it had a massive balcony that looked out over the Grand Canyon. In fact it is probably the best possible view from any hotel room in the area and God let us have it! Oh, I may step out in faith without planning too well but God is not limited by my shortcomings. Hallelujah!

That night we spent more time encouraging Lorrie and praying for her. We actually bought her a meal; we had a meal, too, but it was all by faith as were down to our last few dollars. We just had enough for petrol back to Los Angeles. Sometimes moving in faith is not logical, but when you are in the zone with God you know what to do and what not to do. I knew it was right to spend almost our last dollar on a meal for Lorrie.

The next morning was Sunday. We took Lorrie to the Grand Canyon Assembly of God church and introduced her to the pastor and some of the elders who promised to support her. I watched Lorrie as she sat and chatted with the pastor and one of the elders, sharing her sad story. The strain had left her face now; peace and victory had returned. The trip to America was worth it – even if Lorrie had been the only one we had reached, it was worth it.

Late Sunday afternoon we headed back to Los Angeles with barely enough money left for petrol. That night we stayed with Jim and Francis, friends of ours in Los Angeles.

Early Monday morning I went to check our bank account at a local ATM. I didn't know how God would pay for the stay and for food at the El Tovar Hotel but so far everything he had said had come to pass. So ... would the money be in the account? Or were we really broke, penniless? I can clearly remember placing the debit card into the ATM machine, then slowly punching in the PIN number on the keypad. It asked me if I wanted to take cash out or did I want a balance enquiry? I tentatively pressed the keypad and requested a balance enquiry. I closed my eyes while I waited for the balance to show. Then taking a deep breath I opened my eyes. WOW ... every cent that I had spent at the El Tovar hotel had been put back in. Not just for the suite but for the food as well. We were back in the money again. Ha ha! God is amazing. I couldn't wait to tell Gordon. He, too, was amazed when I told him. The stay in the El Tovar Hotel had not cost us one cent. Glory to God, he is true to his word. Everything he told me would happen at the Grand Canyon happened. Not only that, but we got the best suite of rooms in the hotel and we had the privilege of witnessing the spectacular sunrise over the Grand Canyon from our very own personal balcony. God steps out from heaven to reach just one person if we will just be willing to put the effort in to reach them. On this occasion it meant walking across the Mojave Desert, but oh it was so worth it. I wish you well, Lorrie. Wherever you are now, may God bless you.

Gordon joked and said we should have stayed for two nights...

Chapter 11
I Only Asked For a
Washing Machine

On my return from America Tricia and I enjoyed some normal life for a while – that is if our life can be called normal. We were still living by faith, which meant our income was dependent on God's provision. Apart from minimum benefits from the government to help pay household bills we were dependent on God for all our outreach and to help pay for the upkeep of the many people we were either working with or putting up in our home. He has never let us down. It is not an easy way to live and Tricia had been saying she would like to move out of Ayrshire. The previous trouble in our church had upset us both; we wanted to leave the area but were not sure where to go to.

One night Tricia had a dream: in it there was an evil force chasing her. While she was hiding from this evil force a map appeared in front of her. The map was made up of lights in the shape of Britain. One light in particular was shining and Tricia felt that where the light shone was a place of safety. Tricia woke the next morning and told me about the dream.

I took out our map of Britain. We looked at it and worked out that the bright light, or the place of safety Tricia saw in the dream, was actually right where the town of Dumfries stands in the south of Scotland.

Coincidently, or should I say God-incidentally, I was due to preach in or near Dumfries several times over the next couple of months. A friend of ours, Rob, had told us that he had a house he wanted to rent out and asked us if we would like to see it with a view to renting it from him. He was moving away for at least a year for work reasons. While driving to Dumfries to fulfil one of these invitations to preach and to have a faith-look at Rob's house, we jokingly said on the journey down, 'Wouldn't it be funny if Rob offered us the house to live in rent free.' This would be the only way we could afford to live there.

Well that is exactly what happened. We looked around the house which was a lovely bungalow: it had two fairly large bedrooms and there was a decent-size kitchen and a spacious living room. There were large front and rear gardens and, to cap it all, the house was situated on a picturesque quiet road. Rob, who is a Christian, let us look around the house on our own for a bit, then he came into the living room to see what we thought. We said we really liked the house and would consider taking it. Maybe he sensed our faith struggle, I don't know, but he told us that he had been moved by God to give us the house rent-free for a year if we wanted it. Tricia and I were overjoyed! God had proved himself faithful to us once again. Rob had no idea of the conversation we'd had on the way down in the car when we'd joked, only a few hours beforehand, about getting the house rent-free. So began our stay in Dumfries.

We settled into our friend's lovely little cottage and soon afterwards Tricia and I took in two girls, Tracey and Mary, both of whom were heroin addicts. They wanted to detox from heroin and get their lives together. Most of the other addicts we had been working with in Ayrshire were doing very well. We promised to visit them every few weeks to encourage them and make sure they were OK, that they were settled in churches and living successful, drug-free lives.

Within a few days of moving to our new home I began to work on the streets in Dumfries, speaking to addicts, getting to know where they hung out and building relationships with them. I called into local drug agencies and the police station. I also built relationships with a couple of the local drug dealers – well, they may want to get their lives together, too. Unless I know them they cannot ask me for help.

One lovely July afternoon I came home to find Tricia out in the back garden washing the clothes. It turned out that the bottom of our old twin-tub washing machine had rusted through and had leaked onto the kitchen floor. Tricia is such a blessing – where others may have complained about the situation she did not. Instead, being a resourceful girl, she had pulled the heavy washing machine outside into the garden and had put the hoses in through the kitchen window to drain into the kitchen sink. I was so proud of her, how she always found a way, and without a word of complaint. God had been more than good to me in giving me a beautiful, fabulous and resourceful wife. However, I was upset by the fact that I could not provide my family with a better quality washing machine.

Living by faith is not without its challenges, in fact some of the time it can be quite difficult. We're always having to trust God for something, always having to press into him and present our needs to him for our family and the work we do. Remember we cannot set anyone free. I always have to press into God in prayer on behalf of the people we work with. Yes, we may have learned a little on the road about how to help addicts, write programmes, etc., but we know only too well that it is God who sets the captives free. Only his power and through a personal relationship with him can he release the captives.

I told Tricia that God wanted to give us a new machine. Tricia replied saying, 'We don't have the money for it, John.'

'Well I am going out to get one and I am not coming back without one,' I told her.

I immediately headed back to Dumfries where I called into every charity shop, charitable trust and organisation that helped people in Dumfries. One of these charity shop managers told me about a charitable trust situated just on the outskirts of the town.

I went in to see them and the receptionist brought me in to meet the director of the trust. He was a kind man named Robert who immediately offered me a cup of tea and sat me down in his office. We chatted for a while and then he asked me what he could do for me. I explained to him that I had two addicts living in my home, our washing machine had broken down and I had to get a new one. I explained to him that some of the people we work with have hepatitis C virus and others have HIV or AIDS.

On hearing our story he immediately wrote me a cheque for a washing machine. 'Is there anything else you need for your work, John?' he asked.

'Well,' I said boldly, 'I could do with a dishwasher.'

'Consider it done,' he said as he took the chequebook out again. Now I would be coming home with a washing machine and a dishwasher. I was so happy as I went to the shop to buy our new machines. I could not wait to see Tricia's face when I got home with my new purchases. They were second-hand but they were in almost-new condition.

My problem now was would my car be big enough to bring them home? I wanted to bring them both home together so I could see the surprise on Tricia's face. I put the passenger seat down flat and, with a little difficulty and with the help of the shop staff, we fitted both the dishwasher and automatic washing machine into the car. I had the biggest smile on my face as I drove into our driveway with the new machines. Tricia was absolutely over the moon, especially with the dishwasher. Tracey and Mary were overjoyed too. It was good for them to see God provide us with our every need. We took great pleasure in taking the old twin-tub to the dump. God is good!

About this time a farmer who lived forty miles away had asked me if I could use an old barn on his land, which consisted of two gable walls and a roof that was in need of much repair. I had helped his son in a very small way a couple of years previously. He said that I could use the barn for a rehabilitation centre if I found the money to do it up. I knew a rehab was needed in the south of Scotland, and when I had walked the length and breadth of Britain a few years before I had been praying for buildings. The prayer was beginning to get answered and all I needed was about £100,000 to do the job. The barn had planning permission to turn it into two houses. They would make a fabulous rehab, but where would we get the money?

Two weeks later Robert, the guy who had bought the washing machine and dishwasher, phoned me up again and asked to see me. He said that his trust had some money put to one side and he was looking for someone who could use it to help addicts in Dumfries and Galloway. 'We've had this money for a while now, John,' he told me, 'but we could not find anyone who could work with addicts ... that is until you came along. Do you have any idea how we could use this money?'

Now to say I was excited is an understatement. This was nearly too good to be true. I tried to look composed as I related the story of the farmer and the barn. We arranged to visit the property the very next day; the farmer showed us around. Robert was impressed with what he saw. That week Robert talked to his trustees and within a couple of weeks he gave me all the money to fix up the barn and, on top of that, he gave us £10,000 to buy new furniture for it. To this day I can still remember the look on Tricia's face when I told her what had happened – she was a picture. Yet it was nothing compared to the look on her face when she was given the £10,000 to buy the furniture for the new rehab. She was in shopping heaven.

So began the Walking Free rehabilitation centre. In no time at all it was up and running. I got staff from among my old friends and networked with other friends to help us get government funding. We secured over £220,000 a year funding for the running of the centre and staff wages. We also opened a couple of second-hand furniture shops that Tricia managed, to raise further funds. God was blessing the work again.

I am blown away by what God did during that time. God's faithfulness and provision to us and through us was nothing short of miraculous. Hindsight is a perfect science and I learned a lot about myself during these times too. I know I am a pioneer, I am a starter-upper – that's what I call myself – I am definitely not a maintainer. Often people with my background, that is a background of dysfunction, addiction, alcoholism and homelessness, are not well equipped to maintain projects that demand strict administration. I learned that the hard way over the years, and I am grateful for the amazing administration staff and volunteers that God brought to us over the years.

More Rehabs

During this time I had been preaching up in Aberdeen and I was still carrying the cross for short distances in different places. Mostly, though, I concentrated on working with the rehabilitation centres. When I walked the length and breadth of Britain, I prayed for buildings for rehabs. God was answering these prayers – sometimes we need to be careful what we pray for...

Incredibly, on one of my trips to Aberdeen I was offered the use of a house on a country estate in Maryculter, near Aberdeen.

Remember Sophie, the girl we prayed for just before I had my trip to heaven? Her parents managed this centre and they took in girls with addiction problems. Together with their church in Aberdeen they set up a charity and the second rehab in Scotland opened. This one was for girls. At the time there was not one bed available for the rehabilitation of female addicts in Scotland. This was a disgrace. Thank God for the opportunity to help some girls.

Then at the same time, friends on an island called Papa Stour, a beautiful island north-west of Shetland mainland, offered their home as another rehab. There are no shops, pubs and only one road on this island: the perfect place for a rehab! God was answering prayer quickly, very quickly.

I have learned over the years that if we are going to pray big prayers we also need to be part of the answer to those big prayers. This was my moment, heaven was moving on behalf of the lost and addicted and I had to act. I agreed to do all rehabs at once. So began a hectic schedule for Tricia and me. Staff had to be trained, buildings refurbished, policies and procedures done, risk assessments carried out, and so on. I networked again with my friends and raised all the money needed to run these centres; most of it came through government funding. Our annual budget had grown from almost nothing to three quarters of a million pounds in a very short space of time.

Thank God for great administrators. Between the trust in Dumfries, the church in Aberdeen and my friends on the little Shetland island, they managed the projects. Together with Tricia, I was the pioneer; they were the maintainers. My schedule was hectic. I would spend one week in Dumfries, the next in Aberdeen, and the next in Shetland. This was not without its struggles. Without God's grace, I could never have done it.

Chapter 12
Local Opposition

Anyone setting up Christian rehabilitation work, or indeed any effective Christian work, had better be ready for opposition. I have learned how to recognise and deal with people through whom opposition comes. People will show real hatred towards you, they will malign and accuse you of anything that will further their cause. They will gather people around them to assist them in furthering their crusades. That cause is to try to destroy you and the work you are doing. They unwittingly align themselves in opposition to you and become pawns in Satan's hand. His ultimate goal of course is to rob God of credit or glory by attempting to hinder, stop or destroy his work.

I have witnessed the exact moment when people have succumbed to being recruited by the enemy of our souls. I have literally seen their faces and posture change before my eyes as they turn from being nice, civil people into malicious people with ungodly intent. Sometimes their faces take on a hard, twisted appearance for the duration of their time being used like this. Then they are ready to be used by the powers of darkness, they become filled with hatred and malice towards you. It is quite startling to witness the transformation that takes place in them during this time. Then, they dress themselves in the armour of darkness and they are off on their crusade to try to destroy you. Often these people are Christians; at least we think they are Christians, that's not for us to judge though.

However, one thing I am sure about is that they never succeed in their evil quest. If we stay humble and in God's will their attempts to destroy us will always be thwarted.

I have experienced people give me a standing ovation one week and the next week they have tried to destroy me. Indeed it is not over the top to say that some of these people would rejoice in seeing our destruction. I feel sorry for them, it's so sad to see people come into our lives turn around to be used to try to destroy us. There are many examples in the Bible of people who were used like this. The sad truth is that in the end they are always the ones to lose out. We must always examine ourselves and keep close to God during these times, looking for areas where we may be wrong and be ready to apologise or ask for forgiveness when necessary. This is humbling, but it is good for us and necessary for coming through to victory.

We must move in total forgiveness towards them which may not be easy but is the number-one priority for us to work at: completely and absolutely forgiving them, and praying for God's grace and mercy for them. Anything less than total forgiveness towards them will lead to torment for us during and after the trial. You know you have forgiven them when you genuinely feel sorry for them and find yourself automatically praying for their recovery.

To be a successful pioneer you must be dead to both the praises and the accusations of man. You must know how to press on in the face of opposition and wait till they overdo it and become victims of their own malice. There always comes a point when they take a step too far and they literally shoot themselves in their own feet. Then, shortly after that, the game is up and the victory is ours. We must remember, though, that if necessary and if they will allow us to, we must be ready to step in to pick them up and restore them. That's how it works.

We see many examples of this in the Bible: when Judas betrayed Jesus; Haman's plot to destroy the Jews in the book of Esther. Both of them ended up being destroyed as a direct result of their evil plans and, of course, the work of God continued.

This is exactly what happened while we set up the rehabs in Scotland.

The locals did not take too kindly to me setting up rehabs. I can understand their concerns about having a rehab close to where they live. They may think or believe that drug dealing or drug wars may start in their neighbourhood. However, these beliefs are based on ignorance. We try to talk to people and address their fears but unfortunately, in my experience, once these people are against you, they don't stop until God causes them to stop.

This is how it works: the enemy usually recruits an influential person in the area to head up the attack. They will be the generals under Satan to lead it and they, in turn, will recruit others to join them in their quest. I wondered if it would happen in Scotland and who that person might be.

It wasn't long before I was to find out: it was the local reverend. He was the man on this occasion to come against me. I buckled down for the fight.

Sadly, the local reverend took on the task of trying to get me off Papa Stour, the island where the Shetland rehab was situated. He managed to get in touch with the hotel owner that lived near our other centre in Dumfries and Galloway. Together they tried every way imaginable to stop me.

They went so far as to hire an investigative journalist to try to find some way of destroying my character. He went to Ayrshire to speak to some of the people that had come against me, but by now the rumours had been proven to be lies so, try as they did, they were unsuccessful.

Then they went to the media to try to stop me. Just about every Scottish tabloid paper – and local ones too – spoke negatively about me. On one trip to Shetland there was a helicopter flying around taking pictures of me and the centre. It seemed as if the whole country was talking about it at one stage. Some of the headlines read, 'Former Junkie John Edwards setting up rehab in Scotland' and 'John Edwards has a criminal record!' Like it was a revelation or something! I mean I tell my life story everywhere, I don't hide my past. But, God has transformed me. It is hard for the media to get something on you when you tell the whole story yourself anyway. They even suggested that if I came to Shetland and Dumfries with rehabs, the tourist trade would suffer and schools would be inundated with drugs and maybe even have to close.

I refused to give any interviews with the media: 'No comment,' was my usual answer to their requests for a story. This of course frustrated the life out of them. The Shetland and Dumfries papers phoned me regularly, and at last they said that if I didn't give them a story they would print a story anyway. The cheek of them! They were now bullying me! I must admit I became a little frightened at that point. Don't forget, this was not long after the hurt I had experienced in Ayrshire; now I had to put up with a barrage of lies from the press. I guess in some ways the episode in Ayrshire prepared me for this.

But I was stronger now and ready for a fight. I prayed for guidance and for a strategy. While I was praying I received a phone call from Andy and Sabina from the rehab on Papa Stour. It turned out that the reverend had come onto their land while they were out and had shot their dog, Bonnie, and left him to die. Yes, the reverend shot our dog – it's unbelievable, isn't it? And to top that, he tried to claim that the dog was on his land half a mile down the coast. He was a reverend but he was also a liar; the ones who come after us like this usually are liars. God had it covered though. There just happened to be a couple of guys working on the new harbour which was only about two hundred yards away. He had heard the shotgun go off, looked up and saw the reverend on the rehab land with a shotgun in his hand. The worker at the harbour rang the mainland Shetland police. The reverend was arrested and kept in the police cells in Lerwick.

This was getting ridiculous! It was like the Wild West, the mad Reverend running around the island with a shotgun. Stop! Hold on a minute here, I thought, this is getting serious, and it's time for me to do something. I prayed that day for guidance and, during prayer, I decided to hold a press conference. If the press wanted a story I would give them a blooming story.

My strategy was to invite the biggest gathering of former addicts that Scotland had ever seen. I called people I had helped from Ireland, England, Scotland and Wales, inviting those who could come to an open day in Dumfries. We erected a marquee, made sandwiches, cakes, finger food; we also had soft drinks and tea. The rehab was spotless, the gardens were neat and tidy. The boys in the rehab were all briefed on how to handle the press. A couple of them didn't want to be there when the press and people came so we arranged for them to go out for the day with one of the staff. Then I invited all the local people for our open day and the press for a conference. On the day about forty former addicts gathered; we were in our nicest clothes and had our best smiles on too.

Just before the day began, I emailed the reverend in Shetland and told him we were having an open day and that he was welcome to come. I also told him I had a word from God for him, which I did. I said that if he called himself a Christian and yet could lie about us in the way he had been, and also lie about shooting our dog, then, unless he humbled himself and repented, I believed that within a year he would be the one who would leave Papa Stour. I also said that when he did leave he would leave running and in shame.

You might think it was cheeky of me to write such an email to him. Remember, though, as a pioneer I have a lot of experience in going through situations like this and I have learned to listen to God in the midst of it. I knew that God was with me.

The open day went ahead and the whole village came to it. We served them with smiles on our faces. You should have seen the former addicts serving them that day, they were brilliant. We blessed the local community and the press; we chatted to them and shared our stories of God's transforming power. By the time they left they could not be in doubt that God sets the addict free and that they would have nothing to fear by us having a rehab near them.

The result was that the opinion of the entire area changed, bar one or two people.

In the afternoon we held a press conference inside the rehab. The press were surrounded by former addicts whose stories spoke for themselves. God had ambushed the press through us, they could not now write a bad story about our Christian rehabilitation work. That week a favourable, though tongue-in-cheek, article with pictures of recovered addicts serving the local community appeared in the papers. That was the end of that.

A couple of months later I received word from Shetland that the reverend who'd shot our dog was chased off the island by some locals who had fallen out with him. They shamed him by dumping a bucket of dog poo over his head. They did it down at the harbour and in front of the other islanders. A local man owned some Great Danes. It turned out that he'd saved their poo for a couple of weeks then he'd walked down onto the harbour pier and dumped it over the reverend's head. I do not condone this behaviour, I genuinely felt very sorry for him. I am sure he didn't deserve that. When he took us on, he took God on; he just didn't know what he was up against. I am glad that Andy and Sabina, the couple who ran the rehab work on the island, were at the pier when the incident happened. They immediately ran to the reverend's assistance and cleaned the dog poo from his head and clothes. They then brought him home and comforted him.

That week the reverend left the island. He has not been back since and his house is up for sale. I think he lost his gun licence too. I am happy to report that Bonnie, the dog that the reverend shot, lived. We renamed him 'Tripod' as he had lost his front leg in the shooting.

Royal Visit

A year later we were once again in the media: newspapers and TV reported on Princess Alexandra's visit to our rehab centre. She had come to honour our work. The same people who had fought us and complained so hard about us lined the roads waving their Union Jack flags as the royal party went by. Ha ha! God is so good; we need to keep our eyes on the big picture. God sees things from the end back, not from the beginning forward. Tricia and I praised God during her visit. I had a big cheesy grin on my face as I watched everyone celebrate our rehab work.

Things had changed for the better. The press once again wrote a very favourable article with photos of the princess receiving a copy of the first part of my autobiography, *Walking Free*, from me. I actually got word back from her lady-in-waiting saying how much she had enjoyed the visit and how the princess looked forward to reading *Walking Free*.

Chapter 13
Back to the USA

I've heard it said that 'there's nowt as queer as folk'. I actually know for a fact that there were several people who were delighted at the fact I did not complete my first attempt to walk across America. What a shame for them. The Good Book says we should rejoice with those who rejoice and mourn with those who mourn. Some people said to me, 'I told you so, John, you took on too much,' or 'You bit off more than you could chew that time.' Others accused me of going for a walk and dragging God along. Well, whatever, I believe that if God asks you to do something you are meant to finish it.

God had told me to walk across America and I had not managed to finish it. No matter what the odds, I was determined to complete what I had started. There is a fine line between stubbornness and obedience. I believe that the answer lies between the mix of knowing and being secure in yourself and your ability to hear God. I'm confident in my relationship with God. Remember, God plus me is a majority. Oh, by the way, God plus you is a majority too! I believe we must be obedient to do the last thing that God asked us to do.

I had been gathering a team of people who were prepared to come with me to do the walk across the States. Twelve good people, each of them strong, focused Christians who were up for a challenge and an adventure. I trained again, running, working out in the gym every day, getting myself into peak shape for the job.

The rehab centres were running well and my USA team were ready to go ... it was time to let go of the rehabs to the team and move on to my real call: carrying the cross and preaching the gospel. By God's appointment and grace we had pioneered the rehab work, now it was time to get back out to preach the gospel. Remember, in my experience in heaven God had told me to take the gospel to the lost and to take the cross to his people. Now at last I was ready to go and do the work of an evangelist. Most of us raised money for our own costs.

We planned to do the walk in April 2005. This was springtime and chances were it would not be too hot. Dan Wooding agreed to do the publicity for us again. My strategy was much better this time and I was confident that we would finish the job. Teamwork is the baseline for success, that's what I had learned. I could not do such a walk on my own. Everything was ready to go, the team had arranged time off from their work and we planned to finish the walk within eight weeks. This time we would cycle across the deserts and through areas that were not populated. I would walk and carry the cross in different areas as I felt God lead me, especially in the cities.

I had a problem though: I hadn't been feeling very well, in fact I had not been well for quite a while. I had regular nosebleeds, my blood sugar would sometimes plummet and I would often shake uncontrollably, especially when I had exerted a lot of energy or when I was hungry. I felt the cold a lot and often had to go for a lie down in the afternoon. Sometimes my nose would bleed for quite a long time, causing me concern. I played it down though. At these times I would have to eat something like a Mars bar or drink tea with lots of sugar. I didn't want to go to the doctor because he might tell me not to go on the walk. I decided to wait until I had finished the trip across America before seeking medical help.

One day, just before the walk was due to start, I was working out in the gym. I had done my regular 150 sit-ups as well as my other training. After doing the sit-ups I got a terrible pain deep in my stomach. That night I passed about half a pint of blood when I urinated. Tricia took me to the local hospital where the doctor checked me. He thought that I had ripped something in my workout. He prescribed that I should take it easy before my walk. Good, I thought, I must be OK, after all he is a doctor and he knows what he is doing.

I continued to train and prepare myself for the walk. Thankfully I had no further bleeding from my bladder or wherever it had come from.

Our start date was 1 April 2005. Bob Baker, my friend from Shetland, and I travelled ahead of the team to Los Angeles to prepare for them coming over. Bob is a retired headmaster and a brilliant organiser and manager. He would be in charge of the running of our camper van. We had hired a big nine-berth RV (recreational vehicle) and it was beautiful – luxurious even – but practical too. We also hired a fifteen-seat support vehicle for dropping off and picking up our team as they walked or cycled. Bob and I stocked up the fridge, got water bottles, put the maps in place, contacted our media people and more or less got everything ready for the beginning of our walk/cycle. Tricia and the rest of the team joined us a couple of days later.

I was delighted that this time Tricia was coming with me – she was so excited. We had prayed so hard for this trip and now at last it was happening.

I received an invitation to speak at the famous Crystal Cathedral church near Disneyland in Los Angeles. A group of veterans from Vietnam and World War Two from that church had heard about our trip and they wanted to pray for us before we started. This was a real blessing to us, especially Tricia and me because just the year before, while on holiday in LA, we had committed ourselves to completing the trip across America in the prayer room at the top of the Crystal Cathedral. Coincidence? I don't think so.

Starting Over

Once again the team and I gathered at the Pacific Ocean on the pier at Santa Monica to start our trip across America. This time I was better prepared. We had a strong team, eleven fantastic people all of whom had a strong and definite commitment to finishing the job. It was like déjà vu, a repeat of the first time, but it was now five years later. I was just as determined but more organised and confident we would finish this time. Persistence is necessary to complete the call of God on one's life. Dan and Peter Wooding from Assist.com did another amazing job publicising the trip; they sent word out on over 2,500 media outlets. Potentially millions heard our stories and followed us on the epic journey.

Off we went, down the same road as the first time. We made our way up through Santa Monica, Hollywood, speaking to hundreds of people along the way. On through Beverley Hills, up again over the 8,000-feet San Bernardino Mountains, then down into the Mojave Desert and on through California. Then we went on to

Arizona, New Mexico, Texas and Oklahoma, speaking in several large churches. Dan Wooding used Assist.com, his organisation, to get us a vast amount of publicity through radio stations, newspapers and TV. Emails came in from people being touched, blessed, healed and freed by our testimonies and the power of God. On and on we walked and cycled, carrying the cross in many cities and towns as God led us.

I had been feeling very tired; secretly I was struggling with my health. I had severe heartburn on and off for several months now and my nosebleeds were increasing in frequency. My skin was in terrible shape: I had lots of spots and pimples on my face, back and body, little red veins were appearing just under the skin around my nose. I just put it down to age and the hard life I had lived. 'Consequences,' I thought to myself, 'consequences of drinking and drugging for so long.' I had resolved in my mind that I would just have to live with it.

One afternoon, as I was cycling through the desert near Amarillo in Texas, my nose began to bleed once again, plus my heartburn was quite severe. It got so bad that at one point I was close to vomiting. I pressed on towards the prearranged spot where Tricia and Bob were due to pick me up in the RV. I had cycled about fifty miles in the heat at this point. I began to feel a little faint; I needed to stop, I could go no further. Luckily there was a little restaurant just up the road where I could stop. I almost fell off the bike and lay it against an old disused petrol pump just outside the roadside diner. I sat on the ground with my back against the wall. My whole body began to shake and I went into a cold sweat. I pulled myself up onto my feet and went into the restaurant to order a sweet drink and something to eat, as I knew my blood sugar was low. I found a seat near the window so I could look out for Tricia and Bob. This was not the first time this type of sickness happened, but usually when I ate something the shaking would stop and I would feel better.

This time it was worse though. I began to realise that something was wrong, possibly something serious. 'My God,' I said to myself, 'I am in the middle of the biggest walk/cycle of my life and this happens. God, help me to finish this time, please help me to finish, in Jesus' name,' I prayed.

My determination did not waver, though I was a bit scared and frightened I might get really sick and not be able to finish the trip.

My meal arrived but I could only manage about two or three mouthfuls before it made me feel sick. Just then I saw the RV coming down the road towards the restaurant. I went outside to wave them down. Tricia took one look at me and saw I was not well. She helped me into the RV where I immediately climbed into the double bed that was above the driver's cabin. Bob kindly put my bike on to the bicycle carriers attached to the back of the RV for me. Tricia tucked me into bed. I was freezing, even though it was about twenty-five degrees centigrade outside. I slept for several hours. By the time I woke up we had arrived at our camp for the night. The rest of the team had finished walking or cycling for the day and they were now sitting outside the RV at a table enjoying the meal Tricia had prepared for them. I could hear them talking excitedly about the events and divine appointments they had experienced during that day.

These bouts of illness happened to me several times during the trip. I also had developed a cold in early March, well before we had left on the trip. This, too, was beginning to take its toll on me. No matter what medication I took I could not manage to shake the cold off.

I must say America is a beautiful country; if you ever plan to see it this is definitely the way to do it. We were seeing some fabulous places and meeting interesting people. On top of that we were reaching millions through media. Yep! I may have been unwell but we were living our dream. God had told me to travel across America and now I was doing it and I knew that this time, no matter what happened, we would finish it.

Dear Mr President

One day while I was carrying the cross along a lonely dusty road in Oklahoma, I had an idea. I wondered if I could get into the White House to meet President Bush. It's amazing what your mind thinks of when you're on the road. I figured that with the present bad press America was getting around the world we stood a chance. Here we were – a group of people from Finland, Ireland, England, Scotland, the Channel Islands and also Africa – walking, cycling and praying for America and Americans. I figured that if I wrote a letter to the White House, telling them what we were doing, we may stand a chance of getting in to see the President. Well, it was worth a try.

Tricia helped me compose a letter to the President; we addressed it to the White House and posted it special delivery. I had been collecting soil samples from each State we walked through. I kept them with me to pray for the States as we went along – it's just one of those things I like to do. I decided to buy a lovely crystal vase to put this soil in and then put fifty mustard seeds in it. The Bible talks about having faith as small as a mustard seed, so I wanted to put a mustard seed representing each State into the vase, fifty seeds in all. In the letter to the White House I explained that we would be passing through Washington DC and we, as a group of Europeans, would like to meet the President to present him with this vase full of soil. (Sounds really cheeky, doesn't it?)

I sent the letter off by special delivery, which cost me $21. I wanted to make sure it got into the White House. I prayed with the letter before putting it into the post box. The rest of the team were making fun of me for doing it. 'You're nuts, John,' they said. 'There's no way that the White House will answer you.'

'Well then, if they don't get in touch with me, all I will have lost is the $21, isn't it? No harm in trying,' I said.

Several days later I was finishing off my day's walk with the cross. I was just stepping into the RV when my cell phone rang. I picked it up, putting it to my ear I said, 'Hello.' The voice at the other end answered and said with a strong, rolling Texas-type American accent, 'Can I speak to Mr John Edwards please?'

'This is John Edwards speaking,' I answered. 'How can I help you?'

'My name is Duke. I'm phoning from the White House. I work in the President's appointments office. We have received your letter and we want to see if we can arrange to have you and your team from Europe come to meet the President.'

The hairs stood up on the back of my neck. I didn't know whether to stand to attention or collapse in a heap. I motioned to Tricia and Bob that the White House was on the other end of the phone. Duke continued to speak, 'Mr Edwards, we want you to know that we at the White House applaud what you and your team are doing in our country. We normally arrange all the President's appointments six months in advance but we will try to fit you in to meet the President as you pass through Virginia and near Washington DC.'

I was stunned: the White House was speaking to me.

Me! John Edwards! I could hardly believe it. I might be meeting the President of the most powerful nation on earth. He spoke a little more to me, I can hardly remember what he said. I was in a surreal world unable to take it all in. Duke then said, 'We'll be in touch, Mr Edwards. Goodbye for now.'

You should have seen Tricia's and Bob's faces while I talked to Duke at the White House on the phone; they were a picture – stunned is an understatement. I realised that anything is possible if we only believe, if we will just step out and believe for the impossible, let our minds be renewed to listen to God for his voice and then act. I was thrilled, not so much that the White House had been in touch but by the fact that it was within the realms of possibility. The idea of me getting in to see the President was now a real possibility. Faith rose in me that day. I had touched something of heaven; I had entered into a new realm, a realm of faith for anything. I moved from one level of faith to another that day.

My energy levels were waning, the sickness, whatever it was, didn't seem to want to go away. I prayed, prophesied, declared the word, did everything we Pentecostals are meant to do to get rid of sickness, but it wouldn't shift. It was both a learning curve and a testing time.

On we travelled, through Arkansas into Memphis, where we stopped for a while holding more meetings, doing more interviews with radio stations and speaking at churches. Fox News was on to us now, too, and they were sending out regular updates on our trip. People were stopping by to speak to us. I prayed with more and more people on my way, leading people to Christ, praying for the oppressed, the sick, the lost and addicted. I often found myself speaking to gang members, whole gangs sometimes, white gangs, black gangs, Mexican and

Hispanic gangs. The cross was a passport for me to speak to them. They would see me coming and instead of anger or territorial arguments for coming onto their turf, they would look at me with respect for the cross, and listen to me as I told them of Christ and the love of God. I prayed with many gang members for God to bless them and save them. God was touching many people.

While going through Memphis we took a day off and visited Graceland, Elvis Presley's house. We were thrilled to see all the Bibles he had in his house – they were in the lounge and in his office – confirming to me that he indeed had a Christian faith.

We looked around the rest of his house: it's smaller and plainer than I imagined it would be. The gardens, though, were huge and really beautiful. We visited his two aeroplanes; they were parked in a hanger just across the road from the Graceland's mansion. The planes must have cost a fortune: there were luxurious carpets, couches and chairs in the living or relaxing room area, and a fully stocked bar; in the bedroom there was a white heart-shaped bed and gold taps in the plane bathrooms. It all spoke of incredible wealth. Yet, when we hear how he lived and died it tells us that money, the trappings of wealth and a celebrity lifestyle, do not fulfil a person. Elvis died before his time; his was a sad death indeed.

The next day we travelled on through the famous streets of Nashville, carrying the cross, praying for many, leading many others to Christ.

I was still quite ill, sometimes I secretly wanted to finish the walk and just go home to my bed, while at the same time I knew I could never do that. I would finish this walk, no matter what the cost. The truth is I was living my dream. I may have been ill while I was doing it but I was still living my dream, travelling the world and leading people to Christ through preaching the gospel. God was moving and I did not want it to stop.

Deep down I knew my body could not take much more; I pressed into God every day and trusted him to keep me. He is faithful – that much I know. He is so faithful.

The White House kept in touch with me regularly, trying hard to find a spot for me to meet the President. However, it just wasn't to be, at least not this time anyway. It's unbelievable, but just as we entered Virginia and came towards Washington DC there was a security alert at the White House. A light aircraft flew in over the airspace of the famous building causing a huge security scare. The President's safety and national security were threatened and, after 9/11, they were taking no chances. Unfortunately, they cancelled all visits in to see the President for the next few days. We had lost our chance, our opportunity to meet the President had for now passed. Duke phoned and said, 'I am sorry, Mr Edwards, but you will not be able to meet the President on this occasion. However, we will look at rescheduling it for you. Keep in touch with us about further walks you may be doing in America and we will arrange for you to come in.'

We were all disappointed but, you know, I was delighted at the fact that I had learned anything is possible; at least I can say I almost met the President. I knew that two copies of my book *Walking Free* were in the White House; Duke assured me that he would ensure one of them was put into the President's hand. I don't know if that ever happened, but the possibility of it happening blessed me beyond measure. I had been obedient to God in doing this walk and in so doing we had reached people from both the gutter and the highest-ranking positions in the world. That was good, that was sufficient for me.

Instead of going into the White House the Walking

Free team visited Capitol Hill and toured all the famous buildings that are associated with America's history. Our visit to Washington was memorable and I believe that one day I will return to see this fabulous city but next time it may be to meet the President.

Tricia returned home when we were in Memphis to do some work and to visit the kids. She was to return when we reached New York and the end of our marathon journey. On we pressed, speaking to hundreds, even thousands of people on the road, in churches and through media. I checked our website as often as I could and saw that we were receiving emails from around the world: Mexico, Australia, New Zealand, Alaska and Europe, there were even emails from as far afield as China and Russia. God was reaching people everywhere. I was so blessed to know that God was using our lives to reach so many and in so many countries. I had one email from a friend, Sally Smith from Largs, who heard me speaking from Washington DC on Scottish radio; she was on her way into Glasgow on the bus when she overheard me speaking on the bus driver's radio. How fantastic was that?

On through Maryland, Baltimore, and then just outside Philadelphia I saw my first sign pointing to New York. I thanked God for helping me make it and for keeping me strong. I had had many more nosebleeds and came close to collapsing on several occasions. What was wrong with me? Was I just getting old? After all I was fifty now and I hadn't exactly taken care of my body during my lifetime. Was my past catching up with me? Maybe something more serious or sinister was wrong. These thoughts and others flashed through my mind often during the final stages of the walk. I had to keep focusing myself, checking my thoughts and pushing myself to keep in faith and positive. Every day we walked and cycled was a day nearer the finish line. Oh well, we were nearly finished now. I began to sing 'Onward Christian Soldiers' to myself as I walked with the cross.

The day before we were due to finish the walk/cycle Tricia flew over to New York from Scotland with my two pals, Terry and Alison Quinn. They came in for the finish of the trip and to spend the weekend in the Big Apple with us. Tricia, Alison and Terry stayed in the city of New York near Times Square that night. I travelled by train to meet Tricia the next morning and to bring her down for the end of the walk. There was no way I was going to finish the walk without her.

We had believed for this walk together and we would finish it together. Several years earlier Tricia and I had been watching television and had seen a documentary about Grand Central Station; rays of sunshine were shining in through the high windows into the beautiful building. I promised Tricia there and then that one day I would take her to Grand Central Station – now that promise was about to be fulfilled. I was excited at the prospect of meeting her there. Tricia had been faithful in supporting me in my journeys of faith and it had not been easy for her, in fact it had been a huge challenge. She had risen to it though. I was so grateful to God for giving me the perfect wife. I knew that when I saw her she would have that incredible smile on her face and I knew she would be so proud of me. I was more excited about seeing Tricia than I had been about reaching the Atlantic.

I arrived in New York, marvelled a while at Times Square, then made my way to Grand Central Station. I hid myself on the stairs and waited for her. I was to meet her at the famous clock in the middle of the station and I couldn't wait to see her. Then she arrived and I could see her walking towards the clock, our meeting point. I took out my camera and took some shots of her for posterity and then came down to meet her. It was so good to see her and, right enough, she had her lovely smile on her and that look that says how proud she was of me. That was good; I loved that morning, definitely one of my favourite memories of my trek across America. God had given us the desire of our hearts.

We hugged each other. 'I missed you, Tricia,' I said.

'I missed you too, John, and I'm so proud of you.'

We had a coffee in the station and talked for a bit, before boarding a local train to meet up with the team and walk the last mile together. I had dreamed of doing this walk for many years and now at last my dream was drawing towards its end. I had completely believed that God had wanted me to do this walk. I felt a huge sense of achievement and was delighted that now at last I was about to walk the last few hundred yards to the finish line. The voices of my critics and doubters were at last silenced; no more would they say I could not do it. It was done; my latest commission was now almost complete.

We were all excited about finishing the trip. None of the team had slept too well the night before the final day's walk. We were tired, too, spiritually, mentally and physically tired, but not exhausted. I was the only one who was exhausted but I think I managed to hide it well from the team. I had lost weight and knew that as soon as I got home I should go to a doctor. We were sad, too. Our long trip was over, and the comradeship was coming to an end. We had developed close relationships, enjoyed watching the miles vanishing behind us on our journey, seen the red arrow marker move daily across the map in our RV as we travelled. Sometimes the journey felt like we would never finish, but now at last we were here and tomorrow we would be at the finish line.

New York, New York

On 10 June 2005 at 9 a.m. we gathered together as a team and prayed just before taking our final steps of our marathon trip across the United States of America. We had our American and Irish flags with us, and the Walking Free banner.

We thanked God for keeping us safe and for reaching out to all the wonderful people throughout the last couple of months as we crossed the States. We then set off as a team: Tricia and I headed up the walk followed by Manni from South Africa, Shay from Dublin, David from Shetland, Bob (the Captain) Baker, Neil our support driver from the Channel Islands, Leigh Craster from England and our faithful friend Nanna from Finland; David and Ann Whitehead, also from Shetland, joined us for a couple of weeks towards the end of the trip.

We walked with our heads high, flags blowing in the wind and with a real sense of God being with us. We were thrilled to be finishing our marathon trek across the entire width of the United States of America. We walked into a small park that was adjacent to the Atlantic Ocean. There were about twenty American flags flying on tall white flagpoles. Just beyond the flags was a three-foot high grey concrete wall and over the wall was the Atlantic Ocean. The last time we had seen an ocean was a couple of months ago at Santa Monica beach. We had touched the water of the great Pacific Ocean and asked God to lead us safely across America. He had been faithful; we hardly had one day of rain, no serious crashes, no snake, spider, scorpion or dog bites, no hurricanes, and no blazing rows between anyone in the team. We had arrived safely, all of the team bar me were well, and we were in unity and full of joy.

We walked to the wall, found a spot where we could climb down the rocks at the side of the wall, and touched the Atlantic Ocean. We had done it and I had finally finished the walk that I had started five years previously. I must admit I was a little surprised at the fact that I didn't feel any great relief or any special sense of the presence of God on completion of the journey. Instead I felt a sense of 'What now, Lord? What's next, Lord?'

I looked at the team, all of them were rejoicing; they had completed the journey and were rightly overjoyed at their achievement. For them it had been an adventure, the trip of a lifetime. They could one day tell their children or grandchildren of the great trek they had undertaken when they had crossed the great North American Continent. We had crossed three time zones, climbed mighty mountains, trekked through deserts, preached in mighty churches and walked through many great cities. I joined in with them of course as we hugged each other, giving high fives and celebrating. There was no one there to meet us, no media, no special fanfare, just us and God to witness our final mile. There was, however, one guy, a homeless lad, who had followed us for the last and final mile. We were able to speak to him and had the privilege of praying with him for salvation. That was the icing on the cake for us.

We ate one last meal in the RV together that night and then Tricia and I travelled to New York on the train to meet Terry and Alison. We spent a fabulous weekend with our friends before returning home to Scotland. The team spent the weekend in New York too before returning to their respective homes. Bob and Shay drove back across America with the RV, returning it to the hire company in Los Angeles before coming home.

Chapter 14
Another Angel?
Captain Bob Recounts His Experience

Drive across America Spring 2005

John and I arrived in Los Angeles on 29 March to start the preparations. We were joined by the rest of the team a week or so later, and the walking and cycling started on 8 April.

I was responsible for driving the large motor home and Neil was driving the large estate car. Tricia was doing the catering for the first three weeks and Nanna was coming out to do this for the last three weeks when Tricia had to return to the UK. The initial walking and cycling team was John, Shay, Leigh and Manni. Nanna and I were living on Shetland and three other Shetland residents, Dave Hunter, David Whitehead and Anne Whitehead, came to help with the walking and cycling for two or three weeks. David was the Fishermen's Mission Superintendent in Lerwick.

A typical day started with prayer and worship followed by breakfast and then the walking and cycling team getting away before 9 a.m. One person would start from the camp site, say a walker, who would plan to walk about 25 miles that day. Neil would take the rest of the walkers, cyclists and bikes with him in the estate car and drop the first cyclist 25 miles up the road. They would aim to cover 40 miles on the bike. The next walker would be taken another 40 miles and then start their 25 mile walk, and the last cyclist would be taken another 25 miles and cycle the last 40 miles, ending up at the next camp site. In this way about 130 miles was covered every day. Neil would also travel back along the route and pick up the walkers and cyclists as they finished their stint. We all had mobile phones and could keep in touch with each other as needed during the day. Sometimes, if it was more convenient, the motor home could pick people up, but as the caterer travelled in the motor home, the main work for Tricia or Nanna and myself was to do a substantial shop for food every second day, and get to the camp site first to start cooking the evening meal which we tried to eat at about 6.00 p.m. On alternate days we would only have to pick up a few groceries.

The evening was spent with the team resting and preparing for the next day. My job as joint leader with John was to deal with all the planning and organisation for the next couple of days ahead by booking camp sites and preparing the route details (with the help of John and his computer) for the walkers and cyclists. At about 10.00 p.m. we turned in. Most of the time we all slept in the motor home but, for about half of the trip when there were eleven of us on the vehicle, some slept in a tent.

Some evenings we were able to take meetings in local churches. Every day the team prayed with folk we met on the road as John carried his cross. Many received salvation and healing. We were also able to speak to the media about the trip and send information back to the website some evenings about how the trip was going. It was a great experience in every way.

We thank the Lord for all that he did while we were on this journey.

After about six weeks we were close to New York and I had located a suitable camp site on the outskirts of the city. The camp site book gave directions off the main highway to the site, but when Nanna and I got to the exit we needed it was closed for road works. We came off at the next available exit, but had no directions from there to the site. We found ourselves going along a road full of shops, downhill and heading for a tunnel that took you onto Manhattan Island. It is not allowed to take motor homes through such tunnels as they carry gas on board for cooking. We stopped the vehicle and prayed that God would show us what to do. Immediately there was a knock on my side window and there was a guy on a bike who asked us if we were looking for the camp site. We said yes and he said he would lead us on his bike the one and a half miles to the site along narrow streets. We made it safely and when we arrived at the site we thanked him very much and he just disappeared. The only explanation that Nanna and I have for this was that the Lord sent an angel in the guise of man on a bike to help us out of the really difficult situation we were in. We immediately thanked God for taking care of our needs so effectively. To God be the Glory!

We spent a week or so in New York. The team went in every day to see the sights. I only went on one day, plus Sunday, to attend worship at the late David Wilkerson's church on Times Square. I had been to New York on several occasions before and am not fond of big cities since I moved to Shetland at the end of 1998.

Tricia had managed to return to New York to celebrate the end of the walk and stay the week. At the end of the week in the Big Apple everyone except Shay and I had to fly home. It was now the middle of May. Neil took everyone to the appropriate airport and then returned the big estate car before flying back to Jersey in the Channel Islands.

The next day Shay (who was travelling with my as my navigator) and I set off to drive back to Los Angeles. We had allowed ourselves two weeks to do this covering just over 300 miles most days, although one day we covered 506 miles in order to spend the next day exploring the Grand Canyon. As I had been driving all day Shay kindly did the bulk of the cooking on the way back. He is a good cook, as were Tricia and Nanna.

We had a couple of days in LA to rest a little before returning the motor home and then flew back to UK at the beginning of June.

Chapter 15
Home Sweet Home

A couple of days after our arrival home I had the privilege of speaking at the AGM of the Association of Chief Police Officers (ACPO) in Scotland. Chief Constable David Strang of Dumfries and Galloway had invited me to speak to all the senior police about the drug problem in Britain. I was still feeling quite ill but knew that this speaking engagement was a fitting finish to my walk in America. They were blown away by our presentation. Incredible doors of influence were opening for me at this time, both at home and abroad. The future looked bright, yet ... something was not quite right with my health: I was weak, sickly and was losing weight; my skin was grey; people were beginning to make comments about my health. What was wrong with me? I was to find out in a most surprising way.

Some Bad News

Tricia and I wanted to increase our life assurance policies and, to do so, I had to undergo medical tests. Little did I know what was about to be uncovered.

Blood was sent away for tests and I fully expected the

results to be normal. I hadn't thought about my nosebleeds or heartburn as anything to do with a blood test. Two weeks after my test I received a bombshell of a letter. It was short and to the point:

> *Dear Mr Edwards,*
>
> *Your blood tests have shown that you have contracted chronic hepatitis C virus, and it is active. You will need to go to your doctor to have this treated as soon as possible.*
>
> *Yours sincerely,*
>
> *Dr John Marshall*

That's all it said. I was sitting in my living room reading this just before I went to the rehab centre to teach the guys. I couldn't believe my eyes. I had always had regular tests for blood-borne viruses and never before had this shown up. I was shocked beyond belief. I called Tricia into the room and read the letter out to her. She, as ever in the face of crisis, was calm. We talked for a while and then Tricia made an appointment for me at the hospital in Dumfries. A lovely nurse called Anne took some more blood from me and gave me a CT scan, then told me to come back in a few days for the results.

On return to the hospital I was brought into a room with Tricia by Dr Jones, a lovely lady with a gentle bedside manner, who came in with Nurse Anne. We sat down, waiting for them to tell me what the scan and blood test results were. I just knew by their faces and the atmosphere in the room that something was wrong. 'Mr Edwards,' she said, 'I am afraid that the news is not great. Your liver has some serious scarring called fibroses on it.' She switched a machine on and showed me a picture of my liver. Right enough there was scarring on it – not surprising, I thought, after the treatment I had given it during my drinking and drug-taking days. They then gave me an examination of my oesophagus, putting a long tube with a camera on the end down my throat. She took photos of the inside of my throat and oesophagus. Once again I was asked to come back in a couple of days.

Tricia and I prayed so hard during this time; we had a tremendous sense of peace and I can honestly say I never lost one minute's sleep as a result of all this bad news coming into our world. God meets us at our point of need. I knew that now I was going to have to focus all my faith in God and his word. The battle ahead was going to take more focus than any of my walks or exploits to date. Tricia and I prepared ourselves mentally and spiritually for whatever was to come. That afternoon I told my work colleagues the bad news; they looked more shocked than I had been at the news of my illness.

The next week I was called in to see the doctor again. I had a feeling that it was serious because she asked to see both myself and Tricia together. On arrival at the ward I was immediately ushered in to see Dr Jones. She sat us down, then without waiting for me to wonder what I was in for she quickly told me that I had veins in my oesophagus that could haemorrhage at any time. There was a danger that I could bleed to death if it happened. I had what is called 'varices'. 'That's what's causing your heartburn, John,' the doctor said. She also told me that my liver scarring was more serious than they had at first thought. 'John, you have sclerosis of the liver. Unfortunately that means we cannot give you treatment for your hepatitis C virus until further tests are done.'

I had been told previously that treatment for my hepatitis C virus would start in several weeks and had been psyching myself up for this awful treatment. As you can imagine, this news came as a shock to me. The treatment for hep C can be very unpleasant; I would need to self-inject a drug called Interferon every week and also take pills called Ribavirin. The treatment is actually chemotherapy. I would have needed to have the treatment for a year as my hep C was of the worst kind. The doctors told me I may lose my hair, my weight would probably plummet, and I would feel very ill for quite some time. This was the only treatment available at the time for hep C. I was not looking forward to it. I had focused myself, though, and had made myself ready. Now Dr Jones told me that I would not be able to have the hep C treatment until after the operations on my oesophagus.

I was upset by this news but by now God's grace was kicking in. On the one hand I believed that more bad news was on its way but that ultimately I was going to be OK. I believe that God was letting me know and preparing me for the road ahead. On the other hand I would sometimes find myself wondering what in God's name was happening to me. The one thing I valued in my life more than anything else was my health and it was being taken from me.

For many years I often prayed and asked God to keep me healthy, thanking him for my health. I had been amazed when just three years before this time my doctor in Scotland had told me my liver was in excellent condition. He had told me that my liver looked like I had never taken drugs or drank to excess. I often shared this fact when I spoke in churches or prisons while telling my life story. I thought that they had always checked me for hepatitis C when I had blood tests. Now and again I came across blood spills or bleeds in my work, whether it was through syringes in people's homes I'd visited, through suicide attempts I'd witnessed, through fights I'd broken up, or just through accidents. Some of this blood I came into contact with could quite likely have been infected with a blood-borne virus like hepatitis C or HIV, so I always took precautions. Every blood test I'd had in the past came back negative: I had no HIV or AIDS. I'm afraid I took it for granted that they checked me for the hep C virus. When I looked over my medical history I discovered to my horror that never once had my doctors checked my liver or blood for hep C.

Now it was too late. I was angry: angry at the NHS for not having a policy to check all former addicts for hep C; angry that my doctor had told me my liver was in good condition when it was anything but in good condition; I was a little angry with God, too, for allowing this to happen. I had given my life to serving God, been radical in obedience, trained hard, set the pace for other addicts and used my life to reach out to the underdogs of society. Now I was sick and any news I was getting was bad news. I battled in prayer to get victory over all my negative thinking.

Thank God the anger abated and I came to a place of peace reasonably quickly. Sometimes we don't understand how God works. Life is a journey and on it we meet many obstacles. I have learned that our attitudes are our escalators over these obstacles – good, godly attitudes of trust no matter what the reality, mixed with prayer and worship, will get us through anything.

I had to have six operations on my oesophagus, one every two weeks. They knocked me out with an injection in my arm, then they put a tube down my throat and through the tube they tied bands a little like elastic bands around the veins in my oesophagus. This would block off the weak part of the vein and cause it to die and fall off, the vein then sealing itself again and I would be out of danger of haemorrhaging.

Thank God these operations were successful and I never once had a bad bleed. I kept working during this time, although I was getting a lot weaker as time went by. Most days I had to sleep for an hour or two in the afternoon; my energy levels were very low, my weight was falling and my colour was grey.

Once the six operations on my oesophagus were finished, I again focused myself on beginning the Interferon treatment to deal with the hepatitis C infection. I made myself mentally ready for it by reading my Bible and praying. Both Tricia and I were in a place where we trusted God no matter what. I understood that my faith was being tested and I was OK with it. For some reason God had chosen to allow me to be tested to a level that most people aren't tested. This needs to be balanced with the fact that there are natural consequences to sin or sinful behaviour. Taking drugs and drinking alcohol to the degree that I did in my earlier life had its consequences – now I was dealing with them and I think that's fair enough. God does not bring sickness on us to test us but our lifestyles can cause sickness. However, we can, through God's grace, apply our faith for healing at times like these. 'Something great must be round the corner. Tricia,' I would say. 'I know that God is not finished with me yet.' I would joke and say, 'You know, Tricia, you cannot kill a bad thing, I'll be here forever.' Sometimes, though, I would see worry on Tricia's face although she was always careful to try and hide it and be upbeat in her attitude.

My family in Ireland was worried too, although I never told Ma the details; she would have worried too much about me. I did, however, keep the rest of my family in the loop. They were all a great support to me. I often spent

long times talking to my sisters, especially Maeve who
was fantastic with me.

Chapter 16
Bad Things Happen
to Christians Too

Dr Jones called the house one day and asked Tricia and me to visit her again. She wanted us to come in the next day. What now? I wondered, hadn't I had enough bad news for the time being?

She sat us down in her now-familiar office to speak to us again together with Nurse Anne. They were becoming like friends to us and meeting with them was a pleasure, even if the news was bad. They had a gift of compassion and I know they genuinely liked us.

'John,' Dr Jones said, 'I'm afraid the news is bad. We have discovered three cancerous tumours on your liver.' She took out an MRI scan from a large brown envelope for me to look at and showed me clearly where the tumours were. I just stared at the scan in disbelief. I hate cancer – I had seen cancer kill so many people and now it had become an unwelcome visitor in my own body. I could hardly believe it. I had often wondered what it would be like to have a doctor tell me that I have cancer – I believe most people imagine this dark scenario. Now here I was, in reality, being told I have cancer, three tumours on my liver. Yet I can now honestly testify that God gave Tricia and me his amazing grace to accept the awful reality of my situation.

'I'm awfully sorry to be the bearer of this bad news, John,' Dr Jones said. Tricia took hold of my hand and held it tightly. I calmly thanked the doctor for being honest with me, telling her I appreciated the way she was always upfront with me. I could handle it that way, I told her.

'What now, Doctor? What happens next? Do I get Chemotherapy? Do I get my hep C treatment?' I was full of questions.

'We will put your name down for a liver transplant,' she told me. 'We will have to send you into Edinburgh Royal Infirmary to do checks on you to see if you are suitable for a transplant. We'll book you in for these tests and you should have the test results in a couple of weeks. Will that be OK, John?'

'Of course,' I answered.

Tricia and I left Dr Jones' office; incredibly, I was hungry so we went down to the hospital canteen for some lunch. The peace of God was all over us, it really was. I would go so far as to say that Tricia and I were in good form, full of joy, which may sound unbelievable but as God is my witness it's true. I just knew that I was going to be OK. I knew I had the biggest battle of my life on the one hand but on the other hand I knew I would be fine. I just knew.

When Tricia and I arrived at the hospital canteen we happened to meet some friends who had been visiting one of their relatives at the hospital. They came to speak to us, explaining how upset they were at some minor family problem. I told them I had just been given the news that I had cancer and that I had the peace of God all over me. You should have seen their faces; it put their minor problems into perspective fairly quickly. Tricia and I actually had a laugh about it as we ordered lunch.

That weekend we went down to Abundant Life Church in Bradford. We loved the word that Paul Scanlon and the other leaders were preaching and felt that one day we would go to live in Bradford. I was able to share with some of my friends down there what the doctors had told us. It was comforting to know they were praying for us.

Two weeks later I was admitted to Edinburgh Royal Infirmary. The lovely staff settled me in fairly quickly, giving me a bed on the organ transplant ward. Over the next week the doctors carried out all kinds of tests on me: heart tests, lung tests, blood tests by the dozen. One last operation was done on my oesophagus; my teeth were examined, everything was checked, poked and prodded. I even saw a psychiatrist to talk to me about the reality of having a dead person's liver living in me. They thought of and took care of everything. The good news at the end of the week was that I qualified for a liver transplant. My body was in surprisingly good shape for someone with my level of hep C and cancer they told me.

The hospital gave me a little hand-held buzzer which they insisted I keep with me at all times. 'When the buzzer goes off it means that a liver has become available for you. You must phone the hospital transplant coordinator's number the minute that the buzzer goes off, John,' the doctor told me in a very serious tone. 'You must understand that you will only have a couple of hours to get to the hospital when the buzzer goes off, and you must comply with everything we tell you to do, OK?'

'Of course, Doctor,' I replied.

My mind raced to the imaginary moment that the buzzer went off; it was difficult to take it all in. I actually had to wait for somebody to die so I could live. This was not easy. Would that person be a father or mother? Would they have children, a family? How would they die? A car crash, heart attack, brain haemorrhage? I imagined their dead body being kept alive artificially. In my mind I saw them lying on an operating table beside mine or in the next room as I waited for the operation, or maybe the liver would be in a box that kept it alive and fresh. My mind raced, going down every conceivable path and possible scenario. I wondered how I would cope with having a dead person's liver living inside me. This and other scenarios would run through my mind hundreds of times over the next few weeks.

My blood type was O Negative and I was high priority for a transplant because of the cancer. The doctors were realistic with me, though. I asked them to be honest and tell me everything about my health and sickness. One of the surgeons called me into the office for a chat. He sat me down, gave me a cup of tea and generally created an atmosphere for a serious one-on-one chat. Sitting opposite me and looking me straight in the eye the doctor told me some of the statistics. This was like a reality therapy scene. 'One in four people die whilst on the waiting list, John, and one in ten dies on the operating table. So you understand your situation. Look after yourself, get plenty of rest, take your medication and come back in for all your appointments in your local hospital. OK?' He told me that I stood a better than average chance of a successful operation and recovery and, as my body was so healthy from doing all the walking, my recovery should be speedy. We had some more chitchat about the whole process of transplant, and then he finished the meeting and told me they would let me go home the following day.

I didn't find these conversations easy, not at all. My back was against a wall, unable to avoid the reality of my situation I had to take in every word the doctor said. I battled with woe and negative thoughts of impending doom every day. My world was spinning, but the spinner of my world was God, and he had it all in hand. I hung on to God like never before. I wondered how non-Christians cope with the reality of facing death without knowledge of definite salvation or an assurance that they are going to heaven. I knew of some who resisted the knowledge of God so vehemently right up to their moment of death. How could they do it? Be so proud? Considering their situation, to think that their own understanding of God and eternity is greater than God's? What a terrible shock they would get when they instantly find themselves standing before God at the judgement with their eternal destiny now decided. Their refusal to believe in Jesus as Saviour and God would come back on them so terrifyingly. For them it would be too late, a lost eternity would be definite for them. I was greatly comforted in the knowledge that no matter what the outcome of my operation I was secure for eternity. I slept well every night.

Chapter 17
The Big C

In the meantime we had already planned to do a gig in Dublin. My friend Robert Short had been doing a fantastic job training the Walking Free choir. The choir consisted of former bikers, addicts and alcoholics together with their friends and families. We were a motley crew but society needed to hear our stories and to understand that there is hope at hand. Addiction is a curse and a blot on the landscape of our society; someone needs to do something to begin to deal with it. I came up with the idea of a choir while I was praying and walking across the Mojave Desert during my trip across America.

We had booked the RDS stadium in Dublin for two nights to hold the event. We would also have some drama and hip-hop dancers. We believed that we could put a show on that would completely blow Dublin away and give hope to the nation. The plans were well under way and I was scheduled to be the main speaker at it. The event was to be called Making Addiction History after Bob Geldof's Making Poverty History campaign for Africa.

My doctor had told me that I would not be allowed to

leave the country while I was waiting for the transplant. I was in a dilemma; I had paid a couple of thousand euros hiring the Royal Dublin Society (RDS) stadium and other expenses. I had committed myself to the event and now I had been told I couldn't go. What would I do?

I came up with a plan and decided that I would sneak over to Ireland for a couple of days to do the gig. I phoned some people I knew to see if I could arrange a light aircraft or helicopter to fly me to Edinburgh if the buzzer went off while I was in Ireland. I didn't know where we would land the plane or helicopter in Edinburgh, thinking we would cross that bridge when we got there. I guessed in a field or on the M8. I know this sounds crazy but when I commit myself to doing something I try to stick at it. This gig had now become a challenge to me. I would do it but not at the expense of missing my transplant. I promised Tricia that the transplant came first and that my health would take priority over everything. She was of course very worried about me.

The buzzer was my constant companion; it was with me twenty-four hours a day. I kept it either in my pocket or in my hand and at night I put it under my pillow. I imagined the shock I was going to get when it went off, probably give me a heart attack, I joked. Day by day I waited for it to buzz: one week passed, two, three, four weeks went by without a squeak from the buzzer. My arrangements for the helicopter hadn't yet been finalised but if I couldn't get one I was going to go to Ireland to do the gig and fly back immediately after it. This meant I would be away for two days. It may have been irresponsible of me but I decided to go to Dublin and preach the gospel.

My body was slowing down; the hepatitis and cancer were beginning to take their toll. I was tired and people had commented on how grey, pale and drawn I was looking. I was losing weight too. My body was already quite skinny: my friend Willie Gilmour joked that if I turned sideways and stuck out my tongue I looked like a zipper. I still needed to lie down and rest for a couple of hours most days, but aside from that I kept going as well as I could.

Tricia was a tower of strength during this time and together we found great resolve through our faith in God. We both had an inner-knowing that everything was going to be alright. No matter what the circumstances tried to dictate to us we both knew I was going to be OK. It's amazing how a sickness such as I had brought Tricia and me closer together. We had many blessed times, sharing our doubts and fears and our dreams and hopes. The kids, too, gave me a great deal of comfort and support at this time.

Many caring and worried friends wrote, phoned and emailed to encourage and advise me on what course of action I should take regarding my health. It seemed everyone was an expert on my illness except me. Some people came to me with immature, hyper faith, telling me that I should trust God for healing and not go through with the transplant operation. This, of course, was silly and a bit annoying. I believe this type of advice could be dangerous for younger or less experienced Christians. Emails came in from around the world telling me that people were praying for me. I was sent prayer cloths, prayer bandanas, prayer hankies, Masses were being said for me by Catholic friends, and others were praying and fasting. I even had two or three people offer me one of their livers, thinking that they had two livers, mixing it up with their kidneys! These gestures of faith and support blessed me tremendously. I realised that people are often more kind than we give them credit for. When God made us he put a kind streak in our hearts.

I found that when cancer or other life-threatening illnesses visit us God visits us too. He gives us a grace that enables us to cope with it. We are tested but he gives us the grace to pass the test. How cool is that. My friend Aisling Coyle had done a stormer of a job organising the gig at the RDS stadium in Dublin. Tricia and I had planned to join her in Dublin with the choir the next evening. We were scheduled to fly out at 9 a.m. the next day from Prestwick airport in Ayrshire, Scotland.

At six o'clock the evening before I was due to fly to Dublin I called round to Willie Gilmour's house to finalise plans for the gig. Willie was a former addict who I'd helped a number of years before in Ayrshire. He had become a good friend and worked in the Walking Free rehabilitation centre. His wife Anita, his daughter Lisa, and his son Andrew and his girlfriend were due to fly out the next morning with us. When we had finished talking about the plans we sat over a cup of tea chatting. Willie began a bit of horseplay with me, play-boxing me. I happened to be holding my buzzer in my hand and I playfully punched him in the shoulder. As I did so the buzzer activated, making a loud alarm-type sound. Thinking I had broken it, I stopped play-fighting and looked at it. There seemed to be nothing wrong with the device but then it dawned on me that I had not broken the buzzer. No, instead the hospital was calling me; there must be a liver ready.

Willie's daughter Lisa said, 'John, it's time! A liver must be available.' I was shocked, so much so that I began to shake; Lisa made me sit back down and then made me a cup of tea to calm my nerves. I put my hand on my stomach where my liver is and realised that shortly it would never be the same again. Willie snapped me out of my daze: 'John, you need to phone the hospital, isn't that what you're meant to do when the buzzer goes off?'

'Oh, yes, yes of course,' I answered while fumbling for my mobile phone in my jeans' pocket. Willie grabbed the phone off me, found the number on the back of the buzzer and dialled it for me. 'Here, John, speak to them.' I put the phone to my ear and listened to the ringing tone. 'Hello, is that you, John?' the kind female voice at the other end of the phone asked.

'Yes, it's me, the buzzer just went off, was it you trying to contact me?'

'Yes it was, John, a donor liver has just become available. You must get up here immediately. We have sent an ambulance to your home, where are you now?'

'I'm about seven miles from my house,' I answered.

'You must get home as soon as possible, John; the ambulance will be there to take you to Edinburgh any minute now.'

I was dazed, in a bit of a panic I guess. My friends had to jolt me back into reality. My pal Leigh said he would drive me back to my house. I snapped out of my tizzy and when I did I noticed that Lisa was crying, in fact everyone was upset; I guess it was a bit of a shock for them all too.

'Right, well I guess I'll see you all after I have been de-livered,' I joked. We hugged each other and then I went on my way. 'Have a great time in Ireland with the choir,' I shouted to them as I left.

'We will be thinking about and praying for you, John,' Lisa replied. I was too shaken to drive my car so my good friend Leigh drove me at full speed to my house and had me there in record time. I'm sure he broke the speed limit although I never complained. I was too focused on my dilemma.

I phoned Tricia on the way down in the car telling her that the buzzer had gone off and there was an ambulance on the way to the house. She thought I was joking. 'You're kidding, John,' she said.

'No, I'm not, I'm serious,' I answered.

The reality dawned on her. 'OK, love, I'll have everything ready by the time you get here.' We'd had our bags packed and ready for the hospital ever since I got the buzzer four and a half weeks before. Leigh screeched to a halt outside my house. Tricia was there to meet me and gave me one of the biggest hugs ever. She reassured me and told me everything was ready to go. I could hear the ambulance coming in the distance, the reality of the situation was sinking in. Then I remembered I was meant to be speaking at the RDS in Dublin the next night. What would I do? As quick as a flash I ran upstairs and grabbed my digital video camera. 'Leigh, quick, take the camera and start filming me.' Leigh got the video recorder ready. While he was doing so the ambulance arrived.

I went out and asked them to give me two minutes. Leigh then filmed me as I spoke into the camera. I apologised to the RDS audience and told them that I was probably in intensive care in hospital while they watched the video. I asked them to listen to our choir and speaker and to consider giving their hearts to Jesus and trusting him with their lives. I then spoke to any addicts and their families that may be there and gave them a message of hope. I finished filming, then I instructed Leigh to have the film put on a DVD and to show it the next two nights at the RDS in Dublin.

The neighbours heard the ambulance arriving and called in to see me before I left. They had known I was waiting for a new liver. I was so blessed by the concern and support they offered us. They were in tears as we were leaving. Tricia and I climbed into the waiting ambulance; the kind paramedic sat us in two upright seats, put the seatbelts around us and then we headed off on the one-

and-a-half-hour journey to Edinburgh Royal Infirmary.

I had lots to do in the ambulance. I had to find another speaker to replace me at tomorrow night's outreach in Dublin. I still had to organise bed-and-breakfast accommodation for a few of the choir members. Lots of last minute organisation that I would now be unable to do tomorrow had to be taken care of.

I managed to get through all the final organisation details whilst in the ambulance. My friends in Ireland were so helpful; they took the whole burden from me. Meanwhile we were speeding along the M74 on our way to Edinburgh, blue lights flashing, siren sounding, clearing a way for me to get to hospital for a second chance at life.

I spent the last half hour in the ambulance chatting to Tricia and thinking about the family that had just lost a loved one. Whose liver would I be getting? I so wanted no one to be in mourning, no kids crying, no wife or husband to be sad. I prayed for them.

I know it's silly but the truth is I felt a little bit responsible for their death, like I was taking advantage. I found myself touching my belly again. Soon another person's liver would be in there. I, too, was feeling a death sentence on a part of me. Strange, but somehow I would never be the same again. Unsettling questions arose in my mind: where had my new liver been before? Was the person who had it been a good person? Were they well travelled? Were they Scottish, English – where were they from? Had the liver been in Ireland before? Was it in good condition? Were they a Christian? So many weird thoughts went through my mind. Then, suddenly, we were entering the hospital gates.

The ambulance pulled up to the front door of the transplant unit at Edinburgh Royal Infirmary. The crew opened the door for us to get out. They offered me a wheelchair to take me into the hospital but I declined, preferring to walk. The walk through the hospital corridor was surreal, like I was walking in a twilight zone: lights seemed to be very bright, sounds in the corridors echoed in the late-night hospital emptiness. Tricia held my hand. The paramedics carried our bags to the waiting porters by the lift that would bring me up to the transplant ward.

Somewhere upstairs my new liver was being kept artificially alive, it was waiting for my life to receive it. I imagined a spotless new silver-coloured bucket at the surgeon's feet waiting to receive my cancerous hepatitis C infected liver. I pinched myself to see if I was dreaming.

We arrived at the ward, the same one where I'd had my tests done several weeks earlier. The transplant ward was quiet, lights were low, and most of the other patients were asleep. The staff nurse on duty met me. 'Hello, John, we have a room for you to prepare yourself in, come this way.'

Tricia and I were shown to my room. The staff nurse gave me a hospital gown to change into, but first I had to have a shower and wash myself in a nasty brown substance in preparation for the operation. I was told I would have the operation at six o'clock in the morning. Nurses and surgeons began to come and go in my room, doing all sorts of tests and scans on me. I was given something to help me relax, not that I was too tense. On the contrary, Tricia and I had an incredible peace about us; God had met with us. His peace in us was incredible ... my God and Father had met us like a dad and comforted us at our time of need.

I managed to sleep for a while; Tricia dozed in the chair next to me. We felt so close during the hours preceding the operation; I would have been so lonely on my own but Tricia, with her strong reassuring smile, lavished love on me as only she can do. I was blessed.

More Bad News

The surgeon came to see me about an hour before I was due to go down for the operation. I was counting down the minutes, feeling nervous yet believing my life was in God's hands. Our faith had been tested to the limit. I was thinking about my past life. Yes, it had been hard, with over twenty years of drug and alcohol abuse, being in mental homes, living on the streets, being abused in many ways, losing many of my friends to addiction, suicide, murder and AIDS. Now I had hep C and cancer. The fact that I would soon have a liver transplant was just about as much as I could take. Surely everything would go smoothly now; surely there would be no more bad news.

Just then the head surgeon walked into our room looking very serious. 'John,' he said, 'I am afraid I have some more bad news for you. We have looked closely at the scan that we did on your arrival and we believe we may have found another tumour on your liver. That would make it four tumours, John,' he said. 'I am afraid that it is law that we are not allowed to do a transplant operation if there are more than three tumours on your liver. The chances of the cancer having spread to other parts of your body are too high.'

I was stunned. 'What do you mean you can't operate? I'm all prepared for the operation and ready to go.' Tricia sat by my side on the bed, the room swirled around me, I felt a little dizzy for a moment. This news was bad; I wasn't expecting it and it knocked the wind out of me.

I fell into silence trying to compose myself. I closed my eyes and prayed a silent prayer, telling God that I trusted him no matter what. Tricia was holding my hand and whispering encouraging words in my ear. Slowly my peace returned to me. The doctor was still standing at the end of my bed, not saying a word, just watching me. 'What will we do, Doctor? I asked. 'What are the options? Will I need chemotherapy?' I fired off lots of questions at him.

The doctor replied calmly, 'We will open you up, John, just as though we were going to go ahead with the operation and take a look at your liver. Should we see the four tumours on your liver we will have to sew you back up again and look at alternative treatments for you.'

'Right then, Doctor,' I said, 'let's do it. I believe I will be fine; my life is not over yet. God has a plan for me and it's not over, I will live and I will be OK! I just know it, Doctor.'

His face literally brightened up when he saw my attitude. 'OK, John, let's do it then,' he said. 'I'll go and prepare and I'll see you downstairs soon.' With that he walked out of the room.

Immediately a text came through on my phone from Ian and Wendy Black, friends of ours. The text quoted a Bible verse from Psalms, it read: '"I will not die but live, and will proclaim what the LORD has done." Keep strong, John, for you will be fine, we're praying for you.'

I was amazed: this word came at exactly the right moment, not a second too early or a second too late. God watches over his word to perform it. Both Tricia and I felt that I would be fine. The circumstances called for stress, worry and woe but we were in total peace again. I knew that God was with us, and that was all we needed.

Tricia and I talked about the test of faith we were going through and were amazed at how God met us at our time of need and not a moment before. You would imagine that you would be totally stressed at times like these but if we trust God he meets us as we have need of him.

The time came for us to go downstairs for the operation. Two male nurses gently lifted me onto a trolley. Tricia took my hand as we left the room and held it tight while she walked beside me. The male nurses wheeled me down the corridor towards a big silver elevator. We were all silent, like there was something sacred about this moment. The big double doors of the lift opened, they wheeled me in, then the doors closed again with a *thunk*. The lift began its descent to the basement. I looked at Tricia; she looked back at me, smiled and squeezed my hand. We were strong, nothing could touch us now. We had passed the test of faith. The lift came to a slow and gentle halt at the basement floor. When the doors opened the nurses wheeled me out and down a long, echoing, beige, anonymous corridor. We approached a set of double doors, Tricia still holding my hand tight, willing me to be OK.

One of the nurses then told us that Tricia could not come any further. We were surprised, as we thought that she could come as far as the entrance to the operating theatre. This was an abrupt parting, unexpected. 'It's OK, John, don't worry,' Tricia said. 'You go on now and I'll see you in a few hours.' With that she bent down and kissed me on the lips. I choked back a tear. It occurred to me that I might not see her again; the reality was that I could die during this operation. I loved her so much, wished I could say meaningful words that would hold her and keep her strong. The nurses then pushed me through the double doors. As I glanced back at Tricia, her eyes were filling up. 'Hallelujah! I'll, see you in a few hours,' I whispered back to her. She waved, and then the doors closed, blocking her from my view.

Before I had a chance to become even more upset I was wheeled into a surprisingly narrow, long room. An anaesthetist greeted me. He was kitted up in operating clothes, syringe in his hand, ready to go to work. 'Hello, John,' he said in greeting me, 'I'm going to give you an injection to help you sleep.' He immediately began the process and before I knew it I was out for the count.

Tricia tells me she went back upstairs to the hospital relatives' room she was to stay in for the next week or so while I recovered. She phoned our families and friends from there, to update them on what was going on. She also kept up our video diary of events. She then went to bed and slept for a few hours while I was in the operating theatre.

The operation took ten hours, during which time the surgeons opened me up to examine my liver, expecting to find four tumours on my liver but, to their utter surprise and amazement, there were absolutely no traces whatsoever of any cancerous tumours on my liver. To this day they have not been able to give me an explanation as to what happened to the three or four tumours ... but gone they were.

However, after a thorough examination of my liver the surgeons decided that it was in a very bad condition – in fact they said it was pickled from all the drugs and drink, and scarred from the hepatitis C virus. They decided to remove my diseased liver and replace it with a healthy liver from a sixty-two-year-old Scottish man who had died in the hospital just hours earlier.

I woke up in intensive care ten hours later.

I remember clearly hearing Tricia whispering in my ear while I was coming round from the anaesthetic: 'The operation has been a great success; you've got a new and healthy liver inside you now, John.'

Tears were streaming down my face as I awoke; I lifted my hands to heaven and thanked God for his goodness to us. I had tubes coming out of every bit of my body, including several big tubes in my jugular vein, nose, mouth, as well as other unmentionable places. We were delighted, happy to be alive; I had survived and all would be well.

Tricia's sister Geraldine was there too, she had our video camera rolling recording this special moment for me to watch later. An hour later they took the tube that helped me breathe out of my mouth so that I could talk. The first thing I did was share my testimony with the nurse in intensive care. She actually broke down crying as I related what God had done in my life – God touched her. Tricia told me later that day that the gig in Ireland had gone really well: hundreds of people had turned up and over forty people had committed their hearts to Christ during it. That is just so cool – during my operation lives were being touched and changed. Come on!

Chapter 18
Liver Transplant Recovery

I was determined to be out of hospital as soon as possible. After two days I was moved from intensive care and put into the high dependency ward, only taking morphine long enough to keep the dreadful pain away. I wasn't taking any chance of becoming addicted to the hospital drugs or of growing fond of them.

I had a huge scar with lots of big metal staples in it all across my middle and up to my chest bone; it looked like a shark bite. I was up and walking in three days. The first steps I took were so painful, just from my bed to the shower, about fifteen paces. It took more effort to walk those fifteen paces than walking across America! I set targets for myself, for example I did laps of the wards, going so far one day that I got lost. I had to get directions back, getting a little cheer from the staff and other patients when I returned.

I got many cards and flowers sent to me, so many that I had to put them all round the ward; they really brightened up the place. Friends came from everywhere to visit me, even from Ireland. I had a TV, phone and Internet machine attached to my bed which enabled me to stay in touch with family and friends; well-wishers contacted me from right around the world. All this attention and love helped to speed my recovery.

Tricia stayed by my side every day, only taking a break at my insistence.

Once I was well enough I began to visit other sick people, reading psalms and other Scriptures to them, and praying for many too. They found it a great comfort and I found great pleasure in leading some to Christ during my stay.

One of the patients told me about a sporting event that was unique to transplant patients: The Transplant Games. I checked these games out on the Internet and found that the Ireland National Transplant Games were to be held in Ireland eleven months later. I got in touch with the organisers and expressed my desire to run in the Games. To my surprise they accepted me on condition I got permission from my doctors. This would give me something to aim for and get me fit again.

Thirteen days later I was allowed home. Tricia and I went to Largs, the town I had first met her in, and stayed at the hotel where I had officially asked her to be my wife. I was still very ill and had to go round in a wheelchair most of the time but it was good to be out of hospital. We then stayed at our friends Terry and Alison's beautiful house for a couple of weeks. They looked after us so well, waiting on us hand and foot.

Return Home

My recovery continued, thankfully without any compli-cation. The doctors had advised me to stay off work for a long time, up to a year – or longer if necessary – to give myself the best chance of a full recovery. I was still on a lot of medication and the side effects were not pleasant – in fact they were terrible. I was quite depressed, my moods were swinging one way and then the other. It was a hard time, both for me and for Tricia too. She had to put up with my moods. The doctors assured me that the worst of these side effects would be reduced significantly over the next couple of months. I was taking a cocktail of immuno-suppressant pills, antibiotics and painkillers, about twenty pills a day to begin with.

The doctors strongly advised me to take antidepressants; Tricia too encouraged me to think about taking them, but I was determined not to. I had seen them cause too much grief in many of my friends and I couldn't honestly say that I saw them help in any great way. I was determined to only take pills that were absolutely necessary – I had not forgotten my near-fall from grace with medication a few years before.

I believed that I could rise above my moods through prayer and self-discipline. I found strength through the scripture that said, 'His divine power has given us every-thing we need for a godly life through our knowledge of him who called us by his own glory and goodness' (2 Peter 1:3). I got so much encouragement from the fact that I am a partaker of the Divine nature and not just human nature.

Daily I battled to overcome my depression and one day, whilst with my friends Terry and Alison on holiday, I got a breakthrough. From that point on I was in great victory. I was so pleased that I didn't have to take antidepressants. I knew that even if I had taken them I would have to face the reality of having a new liver that wasn't mine when I came off them. What would I do then when hard times came? Take more antidepressants? No, I couldn't do that. It was so important for me to find a place of breakthrough in God that I could call on whenever I needed it in the future. I believe many who turn to pills for comfort have missed out on this place in God. I am so thankful now that I stuck to my guns and pressed on till I lived in the joy of the Lord.

The apostle Paul said in his letter to the Philippians chapter two that he had learned the secret of being content whether he was abased or whether he was abounding. Whether empty or full, I was determined to find the experience of this secret and I am glad to say I found it. I can testify that God's word is true. I would have this fact tested much over the next few years; lots of trials were waiting for us just around the corner.

Tricia and I moved back into the little house we had bought and renovated in Dumfries, Scotland. It was nice to be home, it gave me a chance to relax and to think about our future.

There was still some work to be done in our little house. I remember one day when my friend Chief Constable David Strang came to see me. He expected to find me in bed taking it easy. Tricia opened the door for him: 'How's John?' he asked. 'Is he in bed?' Tricia laughed and told him that I was on the roof of our house helping to put new slates on. David could hardly believe his eyes when he came outside and found me up on the roof near the chimney fixing slates in place. 'You're crazy, John Edwards,' he said. 'Mind you don't fall off now, you'll make a right mess.' Yes it may sound a bit over the top doing this kind of work and me still in the early stages of recovery but that is what it took to get me back on my feet and well again.

We still had responsibility for many addicts that we had been helping before I had my transplant. I couldn't just leave them and think of myself alone. Some of the people I loved were going through really hard times. Tricia and I talked about what we should do for them and we decided to take them into our home, just for a little while. Within a few weeks we had three people living with us, two of them were babies, one six months old, the other was only two years of age. I had to sleep on a mattress in our living room while the mother with the two babies shared a room with Tricia. I coped reasonably well with it although there were moments when we realised that we had bitten off more than we could chew.

Death Threat

Things came to a head one night when an addict I needed to discipline over using drugs threatened to kill me. Tricia received a phone call from another former addict who we had helped, telling us that this individual was coming round with a knife and was planning to kill me. I knew that it was nonsense – at least I hoped it was. I had received threats on several occasions before but it was always just words spoken in anger. This time it was different though. I could see the fear in Tricia's eyes. She ran around the house finding things to barricade the front door. I was still quite ill and not in any fit state to protect us if he did come round. I phoned a couple of the boys, tough guys who were former addicts that we'd helped; they were well able to defend us if need be. They came round immediately. I tried to calm Tricia but the fear in her was obvious. I decided there and then that I was going to leave Dumfries. I could see how foolish the situation was: I needed to get away from Dumfries and spend quality time getting well.

My doctors had told me that I needed to take a year off from all work to enable my body to recover from the cancer and transplant. You know addicts and alcoholics are the most selfish, self-centred people on earth. They often think that the world revolves around them and their addiction. They are not as willing to get their lives together as I was willing to help, so enough was enough. Tricia and I would go away and start a new life for ourselves. We had already been thinking about it but now the transplant and the fact I was not allowed to work for at least a year brought the decision forward. We would leave Dumfries. Our job here was done.

We decided go to live in West Yorkshire and attend the Abundant Life Church in Bradford. This decision would mean that I would have to let my salary go. The rehab could not afford to keep paying me, especially now that I would be leaving Dumfries. The government were cutting back on our funding for the rehabs and my wage could be used to help support the work. That night was a turning point for us. Funny thing is the guy never came round to kill me as he'd promised, in fact I eventually ended up helping him again – such is my work. I got a message sent to me recently from him telling me that he now lives in America and is serving God full-time, woo hoo!

Tricia and I made plans to move to Bradford. We would sell our house and use the profit to live on while I recovered. Tricia's daughter Amanda said that she would be willing to move to Bradford with the two grandchildren, Antony and Darren, once we got settled and on our feet. This was great news.

We visited Bradford several times over the next few weeks, spoke to our friends about moving down, looked for a house to rent, and eventually found one just on the outskirts of Bradford city.

Within a matter of two months we had sold our house, moved and settled in a lovely house in an area called Cottingley, a quiet area on the outskirts of Bradford. Abundant Life Church welcomed us, we felt included in the church family. We got involved as much as we were able, helping out wherever we could, getting to know more and more people.

Transplant Games

Meanwhile, the Transplant Games were coming up and my training was going really well. I had managed to achieve a good level of fitness: I was now running up to ten miles in some training session and although my fitness levels were not what they used to be, they were good. I find that the blood does not get down to the bottom part of my legs like it used to. If I run fast for any length of time the bottom part of my legs become like lead weights. I entered in the 1500, 800 and 400 metre races at the Irish Transplant Games and although the competition was not great I am happy to say that I won. I became Irish champion transplant athlete. I got three gold medals and a silver medal. I qualify to represent Ireland in the World Transplant Games if I wish. I needed the games to help me focus on getting back to a good level of fitness again. So should I sense God leading me to do any more walks or cycles around the world I now know I am fit enough to do it. With God's help we can do all things – that, my friends, is the truth.

Chapter 19
The Way Up is Down

Selling the house in Dumfries was the only way we could afford to keep ourselves in Yorkshire. You would think that we had been through enough in the past year. Surely God would open doors and do miracles for us like I had so often experienced, heard or read about. Unfortunately, though, the bad news kept coming. The side effects were horrendous during this time and money began to run out. I had to sign on for incapacity benefit; this ensured we got some housing and our council tax benefit. We were just about managing to keep our heads above water, barely eking out a living.

One day, while Tricia and I were driving to Scotland to visit a former addict we had helped, I heard a strange noise coming from the engine of my beloved car. Unfortunately it was serious. The crankshaft had buckled completely destroying the engine; smoke was coming out everywhere. The car was a four-door MGZT, only two years old with a personal registration plate. I loved the car and really wanted to hang onto it for another few years. Unfortunately, I still had finance on it; this was a terrible blow to us. I ended up losing my car and our financial state went into free-fall after that.

It was a great struggle for Tricia and me to keep going; our commitment to each other was tested to the max. I don't feel sorry for myself but I must say it was hard to come to terms with; everything we had built up over the years seemed to get stripped from us, to the point that we very nearly went bankrupt. To say this was a challenging time is an understatement. Our backs were against the wall, there seemed to be no way out for us but, thankfully, we knew that this is the realm God seems to work best in. I knew that and was keeping my eyes and ears open for God to make a way for us to start again.

The car was gone so Tricia and I bought two mountain bikes to travel on. We had these bikes for just a couple of months only to wake up one morning to find that someone had stolen them from our back yard. The thieves had lifted them up and over a metal pole that we had locked the bikes around. It seemed that once again everything we had security in was being stripped from us. Tricia and I just continued to praise God all the way through these trials. We even ended up homeless at one stage as the original house we had rented turned out to be unsuitable, too big and costly to run. We looked for a smaller and more affordable house but we just couldn't find a suitable one.

Tricia got a chest infection at this point. One night her breathing got so bad I had to dial 999 for an ambulance. When the paramedics arrived at our house they took Tricia immediately to hospital and kept her on oxygen until her breathing improved. Thankfully she recovered fairly quickly; we felt it best that she go to Scotland to stay with friends to recover ... I stayed in Bradford at a friend's house and looked for a new home for us to live in.

I am sure that many people would wonder why God let

us go through so much when we had dedicated our lives to helping others and preaching the gospel. I wondered myself how we would manage to get through all these trials. However, even though we were hugely challenged, we never lost our faith. We have learned over the years that God works where there seems to be no other way of escape. While Tricia stayed in Scotland I stayed here and put my head down; I was determined to find a way through to victory. I was not prepared to give up until I saw light in the darkness. Little did I know that indeed God was about to do a tremendous work, a work that would soon turn out to be the most fruitful of our entire lives.

Starting Again

My intention when coming to Bradford was to take things easy to allow myself time to recover, and then to possibly go on the preaching circuit to earn a living. I could make some DVDs and CDs, and write the books that were on my heart. But God had other plans for us.

Since coming to the Abundant Life Church we have settled in Yorkshire and had the privilege of helping many homeless people in the area. Once I recovered my strength enough we started a centre to look after the addicted and homeless of Bradford. We had the privilege of feeding up to a hundred homeless every week and shared the gospel with them every Monday night. Our centre would sometimes be filled to capacity, and many heard and responded to the gospel. We even experienced a move of God that lasted thirteen days. Every day many would come to our centre to be prayed for and receive blessing from God. This was an amazing time and I am grateful to God for the experience we had. We have also learned that the way up in God's Kingdom is down.

Chapter 20
What's Happening Now?

Abundant Life Church recently changed its name to LIFE Church. It continues to be one of the fastest growing and influential churches in Britain and around the world. We are delighted to be part of it; at last we have found a church that has a vision much bigger than ours. The senior pastors – Paul Scanlon, Steve and Charlotte Gambil and, of course, the amazing Pastor Steve Matthew – lead our church. They have all endorsed and encourage our work amongst the addicts and homeless. Tricia and I feel right at home here.

My Own TV Show

One morning, about two years ago, I was just leaving the car park of our church when I felt like God was speaking to me. He said, 'John, it's time to do TV!' Well, you may be surprised to hear me say God spoke to me, yet he did! When he speaks to me it's a little like a strong impression on my heart. I have developed a habit to listen out for it and now usually recognise when it happens.

I immediately went home and sent a couple of emails to

two Christian TV stations, Revelation Television in London and United Christian Broadcasters (UCB) in Stoke-on-Trent. Both stations arranged for me to have interviews with a view to having my own programme. I travelled to UCB TV for the first interview. I met with Neil Elliot, the boss of TV there, and he agreed to look into me doing a programme with them that would reach out to and help the addicted and their families. Revelation TV had told me they had no openings for me to do programmes at the moment but that they would keep it in mind if an opening came about.

On the way home from UCB TV station I received a phone call from Revelation TV telling me that one of their presenters who hosted a late-night live programme had unexpectedly resigned. They asked me if I would consider filling the place. I was surprised by this phone call but at the same time was delighted with the opportunity; this was exactly the kind of programme I was hoping for. I accepted immediately. They asked me to do my first programme the very next week. There were only ten days between God saying 'It's time to do TV' and me having my own late-night programme.

Most people have to pay for the time they spend on Christian TV but here I was with an opportunity that would not cost me a penny, except for the travelling costs. I was excited at the prospect of reaching countless people through the medium of television. I would travel down to London every week to do this programme, a long journey – four-and-a-half-hours' drive each way to and back from London – with a three-hour live programme at the studio. A challenge, but one I was willing and excited about taking on.

The day arrived for our first programme. My friend Lewis kindly offered to drive me down to London. I was nervous but expectant, I had prayed hard for God to assist me on this new venture. I was nervous because I knew the programme entailed taking live telephone calls from viewers. One never knew what problems would be presented and I just hoped I would be able to answer them effectively and with helpful wisdom. I also hoped that I would be able to operate the computers, phones, etc. in the studio. I am not a very technical person so I was comforted by the fact that the staff at Revelation TV promised to train me before we went live.

Lewis and I set off at 4 p.m. on our four-and-a-half-hour journey to the studios in London; the weather was bad, very windy and lashing rain. A couple of hours into our journey a thunder storm erupted, lightning flashed across the sky, the M1 motorway became waterlogged and traffic slowed to a crawl for a while. We were delighted that we had left in plenty of time. Lewis and I laughed, 'Typical,' we said, 'thunder and lightning on the first day of our programme.'

We arrived at the studio at about eight thirty, plenty of time for my training on how to use the studio equipment and to relax over a cup of tea before the programme started.

However, on arrival at the studio the expected warm welcome and training didn't happen. Instead chaos reigned in the studio. It turned out that lightning had actually struck the studio building, knocking out the broadcasting of the *700 Club*, the programme preceding mine.

Staff were running around while engineers strived to get the programme up and running again. A staff member called Dan opened the door to us, quickly pointing us towards the green room, mentioning to us we could make ourselves a cup of tea in the kitchen. He apologised for the chaos and said he would come back to me to give me the necessary training a little later.

Lewis and I found the kettle in the kitchen and retired to the green room to await the training and our first programme, *Voice in the Wilderness*. We prayed hard for a little while, then chatted about what to expect on the programme.

I was watching the time; surely they would come down soon and invite me upstairs to the studio for my training session. The clock ticked away, 9.30 p.m. passed, then 9.45 p.m., the programme was due to start at 10 p.m. The staff continued to rush around, trying to fix the problem caused by the lightning. I convinced myself that they must have decided to delay the start time of my programme due to the problems caused by the lightning strike.

At 9.55 p.m. precisely, Steve, the producer of *Voice in the Wilderness*, called me upstairs. He quickly introduced himself, rushed me into the small studio, sat me on the tall chair and put the head mike on. I was looking around at all the computers, TV screens and other gadgetry. I was just thinking and hoping I would be able to take it all in as Steve gave me my training. Just as I was thinking this, Steve stepped behind me, he pushed a button to his right-hand side and, as a result, several screens turned on. There were different angled shots of me on them. Steve made a couple of adjustments, lowered my seat a bit so my head was in the centre of the screen. Then, to my utter horror, he held out his right hand in front of me and began a countdown. He said, 'Five, four, three, two, one, YOU'RE LIVE...' WHAT!?!

The red light on the camera in front of me went on; I was completely unprepared for this sudden thrust into the deep end of live TV. I had *no* earpiece for Steve the producer to speak to me and help me through, all I had was silent hand signals from him as he stood beside the camera in front of me. You must remember, when you're on live TV you cannot look up, down, nor to the right nor the left; your eyes must look straight into the lens of the camera. People watching at home would quickly lose interest if I lost eye contact with them and they would know immediately there was a problem if they saw me looking around, I instinctively knew that. Thank God I had some experience with TV over the years.

I went into automatic drive, 'Hello, welcome to *Voice in the Wilderness*. My name is John Edwards; I am your presenter tonight.'

In my mind I was thinking, 'Oh my God, I have just made the biggest mistake of my life. How on earth am I going to do three hours' live TV?' These and other panic thoughts went through my mind. My preaching experience helped me through the first few minutes but although I managed to remain composed on the outside, inside I was absolutely freaking out. I then shared a bit of my testimony to help me connect with the viewing audience.

Then the phone rang. A girl's voice came through on a loudspeaker. I didn't know what to do – did I just speak, or did I have to press a button before I spoke? I could see Steve motioning wildly with his hands. I had to look sideways at him: 'Speak,' he said in a whisper.

'Hello, how are you? What is your name?' I had no idea if the caller on the phone could hear me through the phone or through the TV or even if they could hear me at all. I could feel sweat running down my back – this was terrifying me.

I waited, anxious to hear a voice speak back to me. 'Hi, my name is Esther,' she said. 'I just happened to flick through the Sky channels and came to your programme,' she paused for a moment. The silence was deafening but then I thought I heard her sob, the air pregnant with suspense. 'Go on,' I said. She continued, 'I am sorry to bother you but I actually have pills in my hand at the moment and I want to kill myself.'

Oh my word! A suicide ... my first programme, my first caller, and my first time doing live TV. I tried to remain calm, composed myself, and readied myself to try and help her. Inside I was screaming a silent prayer to God for help. There were thousands of people watching around Europe, Africa and even further afield through Internet TV. How was I going to help her on live TV? I felt God whisper to me telling me to talk to her like I was ministering to one of the hundreds of people I have met over the years who have struggled with suicidal thoughts. I adjusted my thinking, tried to block out the fact that there were multitudes listening and watching. Then, I spoke to her like it was just the two of us, just her and me.

I thank God for all the years' experience I have had helping the lost, hurting, addicted and suicidal. My experience came to the fore and I am delighted to say I was able to help. She changed her mind regarding suicide, she even allowed us to phone her back after the programme where we gave her some more private assistance. She prayed with us in private and I am happy to say she was like a changed girl when we finished with her.

I finished that call, but now the phones were ringing full on. I took a second call: it was another suicidal person and once again I was able to help them on live TV and have a chat with them off air after the show. Two suicidal calls in the first hour of my first live TV show. Talk about jumping in at the deep end!

Sometimes we don't realise the extent of our experience in life; I know I certainly didn't. That night I began to realise just how much I could help people, all my years' experience living in my own addiction, together with all the years helping so-called hopeless cases since I have been free. All this experience came to the fore that first night on *Voice in the Wilderness*. That night there were addicts, alcoholics, their mums and dads, and many more who emailed or phoned in for direct help. On finishing the programme Steve the producer, Dan the technician and others came to congratulate me on a fabulous live programme. Together we thanked God for his enabling power and for my story.

Thank God we never had to endure any more thunderstorms or lightning strikes during my time doing *Voice in the Wilderness*. We prayed with many people for salvation, addicts were helped – many who phoned in were in tears, broken parents who had to endure watching their loved children take drugs, attempt suicide, self-harm or struggle with eating disorders or depression. Oh, God was so gracious, he touched many in their homes: some were healed, others baptised in the Holy Spirit. One guy who claimed he was not able to read or write very well told me that when I prayed with him on live television the presence of God filled his living room. He said God spoke to him and told him to write a book. The man said that he had never written even a letter in his life. Yet within several weeks of this happening he had written down seventy thousand words in readiness for his book. Amazing! Other stories of God touching people deeply convinced me that God was with me for live TV. The experience I gained doing this programme was invaluable.

This coming year my team and I will put this experience to good use as we plan to create a live streaming programme on our Walking Free website. We intend to have several live programmes a week, bringing help to the addicted, suicidal, depressed and lost around the world. Some of my friends and I will do the live programmes – what a blessing it will be to have live online help for people with issues and for their parents and loved ones. Please pray that this venture will come about. It's an expensive undertaking but we believe that God will supply all we need to set it up and run it. To God be the glory.

I continued to do *Voice in the Wilderness* for a full year, travelling nearly five hours to London, then doing a three-hour live TV programme, then almost five hours home. God gave me the strength, wisdom and energy to do this, praise him.

Don't Forget Where You Come From

I still travel a lot, reaching out to the homeless and addicted in Britain and Ireland. Sometimes we sleep on the streets with the down and out of society; we go and live on the streets with them in both winter and summer. Last year we did one of our street sleeps in Dublin, Ireland, where we slept out in a park near Christ Church in Dublin's city centre. Together with my good friend Liam McNamara we lived with them in this park for two days. Many of the church outreach teams that reach homeless people in Dublin joined us for the event; others from all around Ireland came to give a helping hand too. We had over one hundred volunteers in all, what an amazing couple of days it was.

On the final day we brought 250 homeless people into the canteen of the Irish Life Centre, who kindly gave us the use of their venue free of charge. Another Irish company called Palace Foods gave us 500 lovely four-course meals to serve to the homeless. We had doctors on hand to examine them, hairdressers to do their hair, make-up artists to do their make-up. We gave them new clothes, entertained them during and after the meal. Finally we shared the gospel with them all. What a blessing it was to watch most of the 250 homeless people bow their heads and invite Christ into their lives. Praise God.

Still Carrying the Cross

I have been carrying the cross for many years now, and I have walked thousands of miles with it, praying with countless people for healing and salvation. In Britain and Ireland I often get people shouting blasphemous or filthy comments at me because I carry the cross with me. One day in prayer I felt God telling me to start bringing a coffin with us on our trips. I told Kelvin (my ministry partner and friend) about it; he laughed but was completely willing to join me with it. A few days later he phoned me and told me he felt led to call into an undertakers who donated a lightweight cremation coffin to us. Ha! I couldn't believe it; it's even got the gold handles on the sides of it.

Oh we've had some amazing times with it, seen God touch so many people. Amazingly the blasphemous taunts that we got when we just carried the cross have stopped. Now there is curiosity regarding the coffin, and a little fear of death from many, too.

Just recently, Kelvin and I travelled through twenty-six cities in Britain and Ireland. We carried the coffin and my cross, telling people that one day they will end up in a coffin just like the one we carry, but before they do they need to encounter the cross. This is radical, I know, but amazingly we have met and prayed with more people for salvation than ever before – hundreds of people came to us. It's the coffin that draws the crowds; everyone wants to know what's in it. Usually I carry my flask of tea and sandwiches in it, together with literature for giving away. But because so many were asking us I decided to put a little door, a foot square, on the lid of the coffin. Kelvin fitted a steel mirror inside the coffin. Now when people ask me what is in the coffin, we tell them to open the door and look in for themselves. When they do they of course see their own faces. This shocks them, but it creates a moment for us to be honest with them, to tell them that one day they will be in a coffin just like this one but that before they end up in one they need to encounter Christ of the cross. Many repent of their sins and invite Christ into their lives, all kinds of people: millionaires, homeless, middle class, etc. Miracles of healing and salvation are happening every day through our ministry. God is indeed good, his mercy endures forever.

One day while we were in London, we travelled on the Underground with the cross and coffin. This in itself caused many interesting conversations and even more interesting stares; people stepped out of our way as we carried it onto the Tube. We had to run past the ticket office when getting the train initially, in case they tried to stop us getting the cross and coffin on the trains. Oh, what a laugh we had.

When we reached Covent Garden we got off the train and walked out onto the street. Everyone was stopping and staring at us; we ended up praying with many. Just as we got down near Covent Garden market we saw a street entertainer dressed like Charlie Chaplin: his face was whitened, he had the clothes, walking stick, even the famous moustache – he was a double for the man himself. A crowd of about two hundred were gathered around him as he entertained them with his Chaplin walk and other antics. Suddenly he spotted us coming down the road and, good entertainer that he was, saw an opportunity to further delight his crowd. He bolted out from the circle of people that surrounded him and came straight at me with the cross. A struggle ensued as he tried to take the cross from me. 'Give it to me,' he said, 'I'll give it back in a few minutes.' I let him have it because I saw an opportunity to possibly preach to his ready-made crowd of two hundred.

The crowd cheered as he wrestled the cross from me.

Charlie Chaplin then brought the cross into the centre of the crowd. He began to be a little irreverent with it so I rushed into the middle where he stood with my cross. Kelvin followed me with the coffin. The crowd grew as this battle over the cross continued. I wrestled it back from him and suddenly it was like Charlie Chaplin was stuck for words. I took my opportunity, stepped up and preached a quick sermon on salvation to the unsuspecting ready-made congregation. We had opportunity to talk privately and pray with some. Ha! What a day that was. Charlie Chaplin, wherever you are, thank you for creating a great opportunity for us to preach to your audience.

Oh, there are many stories I could share with you of how God came down and saved so many people time and time again; it seemed like the heavens opened and God came to meet with the people. There is so much pain, hurt and disillusionment out there, God wants to meet the needs of the people and save them.

Are you daring enough to do something radical to draw attention to Christ and the gospel? I hope you are.

We are busy planning our next tour with the cross and coffin, maybe we'll meet you on the way. Come say hello and allow us to pray with you and for your loved ones, that they and you will experience the incredible presence of God.

Family and Future
Amanda and two of our grandchildren, Antony and Darren, have moved down to Bradford too. They live just around the corner from us. Amanda and Michael have recently brought our first granddaughter into the world, her name is Melissa and she is just gorgeous. Life is good, the future looks brighter than ever and God still makes a way where there seems to be no way.

Paul (Tricia's son, my stepson) and his wife Julie have just recently moved down to near us too. They have got a dream job and are settling down well in beautiful Yorkshire. It is so nice having family nearby, they bring so much joy to our lives.

I must say I am so grateful to be alive. We still have our tough moments but the blessings of God far outweigh the tough times. I find that having a vision for my life is what keeps me going. I just celebrated my eighth anniversary since my liver transplant. I recently went through treatment for hepatitis C virus and had to have forty-one units of blood transfused while undergoing the treatment but, thank God, it was successful and the hep C is now non-detectable. Looks like I have another reprieve and another chance at living a healthy life. God is good.

Chapter 21
It's Autumn Now

We now live near Bingley, West Yorkshire, not far from the famous Liverpool Leeds canal. I often go walking down there; it's quiet, peaceful and beautiful.

One lovely evening last autumn while I was walking there I observed a huge slug slowly making his way across the dry sandy towpath that winds its way along by the canal. I stopped to look at him for a while. His progress was slow; in fact if you didn't stop to observe him closely you would have thought he wasn't moving at all. He still had about five feet to crawl before he got to the grassy side of the towpath where he would find refuge, safety and food. I noticed that his back had become sticky; he was beginning to dehydrate in the late-autumn sun. The sand on the path was soaking up his body moisture. His sticky back had picked up small musty bits of last year's autumn leaves and granules of sand on his long and arduous journey towards his destination.

I knew that the slug would not make it to the other side where he could find refuge under the lush greenery on the far side of the towpath. It would be impossible for him to make this journey; if he did not receive help at this point of his journey he would definitely die. I watched him for a while, observing his determined yet slow progress across what must have seemed like a desert to him. I knew what it felt like to be in this position in life. The journey is slow, the destination is still far away, you're tired, depressed and you don't feel you have the strength to make it there. I knew that only outside help could get him to where he wanted to go.

I bent down on my knees beside the slug and picked him up. I then wiped away the debris he had picked up on his journey and gently placed him on the most fertile piece of soil beside the canal. There was plenty of cover and lots of food there for him. He would live now. There is no way he would have made it without my help.

I thought about my sister Evelyn – remember I introduced you to her at the start of this book? She died while I was writing chapter four. I miss her desperately. She fought so hard to live; she had given life her very best effort. God has taken her to a place that she could not get to on her own. He has picked her up and taken away all the debris and hardship that she picked up on her journey and he has placed her in a fertile place, a place where there are no more tears, no more pain, no more sickness; a place with an abundance of joy together with the everlasting privilege of being in the presence of God himself.

Yes, it's late autumn now and the leaves are changing colour on the trees: fabulous rich reds, yellows and browns, all the glorious colours of death on dying leaves. Some are falling into the canal, to drift to an unknown destination.

God has given me a second chance and I hope and pray that I can introduce as many people as possible to the God who makes a way where there seems to be no way. I hope and pray that you will find the humility within yourself to invite Christ into your life so he can wash away the debris that you have picked up on your journey.

I hope and pray that you will humble yourself to the point that you will allow him to pick you up and bring you to a place of eternal bliss; a place where there is no sin – yes, a place where there are no addicts, no homeless people, no poverty or pain, sickness or death; indeed a place where you will get eternal accommodation, joy and freedom.

I wish you well, my friends. I pray for all my readers, that God will bless your life, that he will reveal himself to you and put a song back into your heart. Why don't you find a quiet place right now and invite Christ into your heart. You too, like me, will one day end up in a coffin. Pray and invite Christ to reveal the cross to you so you may find freedom in this sad, fallen world.

I pray you will ask Christ into your life right now. You can pray with me now if you like, I am praying for you right now as I write this simple prayer:

Dear God, please forgive me for every sin I have ever committed. I believe that Christ died for me on the cross, that he shed his blood, died and rose again after three days so I could live for eternity in heaven. I ask you, God, to come into my heart to be my Lord and my Saviour. Help me to turn my life around, to leave my sinful life behind me, also to experience your presence. Heal me from the pain life has brought to me and set me free from all its effects. I commit my life to you now God. Please walk with me and talk with me on a daily basis.

If you have sincerely prayed this prayer I would love to know. Please email me at johnwalkingfree@gmail.com and I will pray for you too.

Thank you for joining me in my story written on the pages of this book. I finish with a short poem I was inspired to write while driving over the Yorkshire moors recently. I hope you enjoy it.

May God richly bless you all, may he become real to you, give you a hope and a future.

John.

My Poem:
'For Heaven's Sake'

When I get to heaven, will I remember the good times and the bad dealt from life's unfair hand?

Will the moonlight shine from plastic needles, filled with poison in London's West End's dark alleys shock my memory with failure still?

Or, will memories of freezing cardboard mattress nights in winter's coldest days still chill me?

Will old terror times in padded cells with fears of destined lunacy stay with me even there?

When I get to heaven will the memory of God's beauty in the yellows and golds from gorgeous dying autumn leaves and green ones hanging, persevering, not letting go, but clinging on to the end of summer sap leave good feelings in my spirit still?

Will I remember wishes made at spring's first daffodils

and will the melody of the song thrush still fill me with joy and good news of summer's coming?

When I get to heaven will the open log fires from Galway bars with oak beams, laughing, and Irish dancing, still awaken warm memories of good clean fun?

Will holidays on Lough Rea island, grey clinker rowing boats, water lapping at their sides, spiders' long legs aiding them to walk on water, sun rising, setting, fish jumping at mayfly swarms linger? Or will mother's hugs and father's bedtime stories still carry comfort to me even then?

Oh, Lord, earth's long, hard knocks and brief moments of smiling times are all I know.

When I get to heaven, will you sit with me on streets of gold or on crystal seas in a clinker boat or better still to walk on it and will you tell me how things really are?

Lord, when I get to heaven will you hug and tell stories too? Or walk me to my mansion on joy-filled streets where old friends and family await my coming home?

Will we fish and run, have fun on rolling hills arrayed in colours unseen on earth's fallen fields?

Will I see you face to face? Will angels play and heavenly choirs sing your praises with me and ... will I be filled with ecstasy for real?

In heaven, Lord, can I enjoy the blessing of remembering the good times and the bad in the light of knowing neither can touch me here?

For now, dear Lord, I promise you that I will live for heaven's sake and take the hurting and the lame to heaven's gate where you will wipe away their tears and help them, too, to live this life.

Will you help me do this, Lord? At least until I join you for eternity? Do please, for heaven's sake.

Other Books by John Edwards

Walking Free
(John's autobiography Part One)

God Help, My Child's an Addict
(This is a book to help the families of those struggling
with life-controlling issues)

www.walkingfree.org